Narratives of
Social Justice Teaching

Studies in the
Postmodern Theory of Education

Joe L. Kincheloe and Shirley R. Steinberg
General Editors

Vol. 332

PETER LANG
New York • Washington, D.C./Baltimore • Bern
Frankfurt am Main • Berlin • Brussels • Vienna • Oxford

sj Miller, Laura Bolf Beliveau, Todd DeStigter,
David Kirkland, and Peggy Rice

Narratives of
Social Justice Teaching

How English Teachers Negotiate Theory
and Practice Between Preservice
and Inservice Spaces

PETER LANG
New York • Washington, D.C./Baltimore • Bern
Frankfurt am Main • Berlin • Brussels • Vienna • Oxford

Library of Congress Cataloging-in-Publication Data

Narratives of social justice teaching: how English teachers negotiate theory and practice
between preservice and inservice spaces / sj Miller ... [et al.].
p. cm. — (Counterpoints: studies in the postmodern theory of education, 1058-1634; v. 332)
Includes bibliographical references and index.
1. Teachers—Training of—Social aspects—United States. 2. English teachers—
Training of—Social aspects—United States. 3. Social justice—Study and teaching—
United States. 4. Postmodernism and education—United States. I. Miller, sj.
LB1715.N32   428.0071'173—dc22   2008003294
ISBN 978-1-4331-0127-4
ISSN 1058-1634

Bibliographic information published by **Die Deutsche Bibliothek**.
Die Deutsche Bibliothek lists this publication in the "Deutsche
Nationalbibliografie"; detailed bibliographic data is available
on the Internet at http://dnb.ddb.de/.

Cover concept and art by Gina Negley

© 2008 Peter Lang Publishing, Inc., New York
29 Broadway, 18th floor, New York, NY 10006
www.peterlang.com

Printed in the United States of America

This book is dedicated to all of the individuals who have been, and continue to be, courageous in making schools a place that is welcoming for everyone.

Be the change you want to see in the world.

Gandhi

TABLE OF CONTENTS

FOREWORD
If We Could, Only, What?

Ruth Vinz

And I Think to Myself....

Some stories stay with us. Here is one that seems fitting for a collection of narratives on teaching toward social justice. This narrative will differ from others in this collection in ways I regret. Only through recollection can I re-create the words and actions of the preservice and cooperating teachers, the supervisor, principal, and university department chair that were implicated in the events I try to describe some sixteen years after they occurred.

The story. I enter the classroom. Spacious and sunny, the large windows frame an early morning view of the Sawtooth's jagged peaks. Judith, the cooperating teacher, is deep in conversation with one small group. Rosa, the student teacher, sits to the side notebook in hand, recording observations. I focus on the student-made posters covering the walls. Each advertises and advocates a position on forest conservation. This is rural logging country, but the pristine forests attract locals as well as world-class white water kayakers, climbers, skiers, and fishermen. The town's economy depends on the logging camps, sawmills, and paper mills as well as its resorts and recreational activities. The tensions are never resolved but the town thrives on its own mixed messages. The cooperating teacher, Judith, prides herself on creating a curriculum based on "Issues" as the organizing concept of her sixth grade English curriculum. Students read about the issues from a variety of genre, including nonfiction. They also research and write about these issues from multiple perspectives. The units range from Discovering Family and Friends, Examining Abilities and Disabilities, Finding Your Passions, and Learning about Others. They are working through a unit titled "Facing Local Issues in the Community" at the time of my visit. Judith has a reputation for involving students in the questions and topics they care about and motivating them to "write out of and for life" as she describes the literacy work of her classroom. She graduated from the same program that Rosa is completing.

I start this narrative with details about the town, the classroom, and Judith's curriculum to keep from confronting the actual story that brought me to her classroom on this particular morning so many years ago. I am here to confront "the box." There, I've said it. Yes, a literal box—a refrigerator box that is prominently displayed in the center of this classroom. Yes, a cardboard shipping box for a refrigerator, cut down to about 5' 10" height with the branding, Frigidaire, in bold, black letters on two of its four sides. Students' desks border it in near the circumference as if guards to the tower. The box occupies a more prominent place in the room than I'd imagined. In my mind's eye, the box lurked in the back corner away from the classroom action and interactions, hidden as much as possible from view because of what I think is the shame of it. But, my imagined box is different from the one I find here. This box, large and imposing, displays colorful drawings on the outside, cut out windows that open wide to create fold back shutters that can shut out the view when desired. The top has six skylights covered with plastic, casting beams of fluorescence to the interior. The door has a rope handle and just above it, a sign, hand painted with intricate animal faces and designs around the words "DAMON'S SPACE— KEEP OUT!"

Judith talks with a group of students about a letter they are writing to the local newspaper. Rosa, earnestly, makes notes, and, as Judith moves around talking with other small groups of students, Rosa joins a group who asks for her help. They are creating a script for a radio play on a recent protest that highlights the paper mill's part in polluting the nearby river, using interviews they conducted as the basis for the story they want to tell. Another group debates what to include in a letter to the Zoning Board asking them to reject an application for a large hotel resort proposed to be built along the river. The classroom fills with animated talk and a mix of earnestness and laughter. Judith moves to the box. She kneels in front of a jaggedly carved window and starts a conversation with Damon.

I try to get a look inside by leaning a little to the left of Judith's head. I see a face peering out of the open window. Inside, Damon is staring intently at his teacher, pencil in hand, nodding until he catches my eye. He reaches for the shutter fold and pulls half the window closed. Judith continues talking with him, but he has blocked my view. My stomach hurts. My mind brims over with indignation, frustration, and sadness.

Competing Intentions: WE Each Know Better than the Other

Why am I here this morning? Rosa struggles with "classroom control." These seem the words that often substitute for more complicated explanations. Truth is: Rosa expressed her indignation that Damon's classroom space consists of a large refrigerator box with a cut-out door and windows. This, of course, sounds ludicrous still as I write these words. As Rosa tells it, she talked with Judith, telling her it isn't right that Damon should be confined to this box, questioning the legality and the ethics of this, and confronting her university supervisor, Judith, and the principal. The outcome of that meeting—Judith says: "Go ahead and try it. You'll see. We all have seen. WE know better than to let Damon out of his box. It's best for everybody." The principal and supervisor let silence be the spokesperson for their opinions.

So, Rosa prods Damon out of the box in the blocks of time when she is teaching. She asks that he work with one of the small groups. Now, a week later, I am here to give a "second opinion" to what Judith and the supervisor insist is a classroom in disarray. On this day, I have been called in to "evaluate" Rosa's teaching, which my department chair describes as "out of control." I am to provide a "second opinion of the problems." The chair says, "We need to deal with this situation (translate that to mean the situation is Rosa). Our relationship with this school can't be compromised. We have great placements and it's a strong research site." So I understand now that my job is to confirm that there are "problems with Rosa's classroom control." The chair indicates that the supervisor and Judith think Rosa should either be reassigned to an easier classroom or encouraged to quit.

Rosa and I meet the day before my visit. What did I say to Rosa in that meeting? Did I explain that my role in visiting might be clearly tied to decisions about her future? I'm sure I downplayed the seriousness of her situation. Did I agree to this visit knowing that decisions had already been made, and I was simply the procedural and institutional pawn to its ending? What I remember most are Rosa's words. Here I try to reconstruct them from notes I kept on the incident but more from how they now reside in the cobwebs of my memory:

> I cannot be a teacher if I'm asked to do what isn't ethical. I think teachers must make choices. So much of what we study in our program keeps coming back to ideas of fairness, equality, and justice in the curriculum. If it's that in curriculum it must be that in the classroom practices. How do I practice with integrity in a situation like this one? Damon has so much potential and boxing him up in the classroom raises huge questions about what I believe and value. Who benefits from him placed in a box? I think he has learned compliance there and so it seems okay. But, doesn't this inhibit his social growth even if one of the justifications is that he wants this? He cannot be detached from and unaffected by others. Judith doesn't seem to realize the treatment of him is opposed to the curriculum she teaches. I think putting Damon in a box is a form of domination. I think no one is thinking about what else to do. What do the other students learn from this? It's just the easiest course of action.

This incident occurred the year I left the high school classroom after twenty-three years of teaching and moved to teaching at the university. I thought I'd heard, read, and seen just about everything; but, not a child confined to a box placed in the middle of the classroom, as if there were some normalcy about it all.

I take a deep breath as Judith calls her part of the lesson to a close. I see Rosa leave the group she is working with, pick up a folder and walk to the front of the room. It is her turn now. For the next forty-three minutes she will transform from her "student teaching" role to her "student teaching" persona. We all seem poised for what is to come next.

I've meant to tell this story for a long time. I've even tried writing it over the years, in several versions that tend to fizzle out when I get to this part of the story. I just cannot crystallize its meaning. I've tried telling it orally and usually it elicits groans and often anger and sometimes right out indignation before I've narrated the first three events. Somehow I believe the story of the "box," of Damon, of Rosa, of Judith, of me, and institutional complicity in this event will serve as a Preface to the narratives told in this important book, *Narratives of Social Justice Teaching: Negotiating between University, Inservice, and Preservice Spaces.*

Much of what this incident can teach is how competing intentions work against our ability to maintain communication across differences, to interrogate practices, to listen to and support those who struggle, and to challenge institutional practices and procedures that may not be conducive to learning. In writing about this incident now, I understand better how each of us was complicit in maintaining our individual perspectives and positions. We each seemed to work from the position: WE/I know better than anyone else. Events surrounding this incident continued to move forward and build momentum while each of us stood, rock-solid, in our separate perspectives.

The agenda, if not the intent, of educational efforts to achieve social justice have changed over time, but central questions remain: How can we work together to think about, rethink, and reexamine principles of social justice and equity in education? How can we educate students for social justice both explicitly through the curriculum and classroom life and implicitly by uncovering and challenging educational practices that privilege, marginalize, or ignore differing critical notions of equality and justice? Behind the apparent divisiveness of multiple intentions and perspectives, how might we promote ethical consciousness that contributes to the educational practices of equity and social justice that will support curricula intended to teach about social justice? As each of the chapters in this book will teach us, these questions can be examined through the narratives we choose to tell, but there is more. The critical turn will be to consider how we use those narratives responsibly to question and critique our understandings, knowledges, and practices toward equitable means and ends.

"I Just Want to Open Doors for Him"

At the moment when Rosa starts teaching, I am thinking that Judith has allowed herself to regularize "the box," and has segmented it somehow from her more typically political viewpoints about social learning and action as founda-

tional in her classroom. I can't put these discrepancies into any logical relationship in my mind. Judith walks out of the classroom as Rosa walks over to Damon's box and opens the door. He retreats and then steps forward. As he
moves through the doorway, Rosa pats Damon's shoulder. He leans away from
her touch. I move to a small table at the back of the room, and before I can sit
down, Damon leaps over three desks. In the second before he turns and faces
Rosa, I notice he has a pair of scissors in his hand. He points them toward her.
The moment is freeze framed. Rosa leans toward him, quietly, "Damon, please
let me have the scissors. You don't need them right now. Will you let me have
them, please?" Damon doesn't move. "Damon, please. How about you go to
work with your group like yesterday? You could help them again with the drawings. Your drawings are the best. Your group needs you."

The scissors move in Damon's hand. Up, down, up again—a small glint of
silver caught in the rays of fluorescence. Rosa extends her hand, palm up, a
place for the scissors. The room is very still.

Damon throws the scissors into the air and takes off, full tilt, using desks
and the students in them as hurdles for his race toward the back window just
behind me. As he leaps onto the windowsill, I reach and grab the back of his
shirt and slide him into my arms in a near locked position. He squirms at first,
goes limp, and I sit back down with him on my lap. My arms tighten around his
chest. My heart flutters at the thought that we are on the fourth floor where the
old windows are thin glass that could break with no more than the heavy thud
of a fifty-pound boy against them. "It's okay, it's okay," I'm whispering in his
ear. "I just don't want you to get hurt." The first thing I notice, beyond the
heart beating in his chest and the sweet smell of peach in his hair, is Rosa staring right at me. There is a near accusation in her tilted brow. I release some of
the pressure of my arms off Damon. He starts to struggle. I tighten up again.
He goes quiet.

It's now I notice that the students have turned my way as if to see what I'll
do. I don't have a clear plan or any insight to deal with this. "Ms. Martinez," I
hear myself saying to Rosa, "Damon and I are just fine here. Go ahead and get
the groups started. We'll see if Damon feels like drawing a little later." I hand
him my pen and fumble, one-handed for a pencil in my bag. He takes it from
me. I don't remember what happens after that for the next forty minutes of
class. The smell of peach stays with me most. In my haste to give Damon some
paper, I open to a blank page in my teaching journal. Now, looking back at the
three pages where he sketched during the remainder of the class, I find prehis-
toric looking birds, insects I can't identify, and exotic-looking horses. Both flora
and fauna are rich in detail demonstrating the artist's mind is brimming with
imagination. Habitats unlike any we could point to and name on a map. Damon
draws and the groups settle into their work; Rosa moves among them asking

questions and occasionally looking back at me. I don't think Damon knows I am there any longer. He has left this world and moved into the picture world he has created in my notebook. He draws, accompanied by the drone of the class-room work.

Even now, I don't have answers for dealing with this situation. I do think we have resources and strategies that I couldn't have imagined then. As Judith reenters the classroom there is an accusatory look as she walks toward us. "Damon, come with me," she walks him back toward his box. Do you need the bathroom now? Mr. Landis will be here soon to start social studies. Do you need a little break?" Rosa turns toward me, "I just want to open doors for him."

"I Can't Give You Anything Except My Opinions"

Fast forward to the noon meeting where Judith, Rosa, and I meet with the principal. Rosa's supervisor joins us. Will it be possible for us talk through and reflect on what we each experienced? Our competing understandings, values, and personal experiences are the boxes around us that help us describe and in-terpret "the box" in the classroom. And behind the talk of "boxes," the lives of Damon and Rosa seem those most affected by what others make of this situa-tion.

If the box is about a literal space of contention, it is also a metaphor that demonstrates how easily walls are erected to keep us separate and/or protected (depending on individual perspectives). I learn in this meeting that Judith is more uncertain than she appears. This is the second year her school has been "inclusive." Judith describes the lack of resources and professional development that might help her work with students who have a unique set of challenges. She feels that the teachers are expected "to deal" without the benefit of even a special education expert or other knowledge resources in the school.

The principal describes the origins of the idea of the box. I learn that Da-mon's mother suggested "the box" because he crawls into small spaces at home and his father constructed several little rooms within the house that provide him more safety and less stimulation. "I can't give you anything but my per-sonal opinion," Damon's mother told the principal over and again. The princi-pal expresses his enthusiasm for the suggestion and goes so far as to take a Sat-urday morning trip to a local appliance store where he acquires the box. He re-minds our group that this solution seems to satisfy everyone except Rosa.

Rosa speaks up and expresses how astonished she was when she first en-tered the classroom. "A box with a sixth grade boy in it. I thought there was a role-play going on or something like that. How could this boy be physically po-sitioned in this way and separated from his classmates? I still can't believe it." No one answers her directly. The corporeal gestures speak louder than words.

Judith describes Damon's "issues" as best she understands them. I learn that Damon is diagnosed as autistic. He is labeled, and teachers are expected to know how to help him within this world of school where identified/"identitied" human beings are treated according to their labels. I wonder when and how the label substitutes for the name, Damon, and, hence, the human being? I ask this. Foreheads bow toward the table. No response except a furious nod of affirmation from Rosa.

Many thoughts travel through my mind. How, I wonder, did Judith get either desensitized or sensitized differently to accept how this practice might be a necessary or productive one? And, I'm certain Judith questions Rosa's and my positions as well. How much pressure did the principal and mother exert on Judith's decisions, and, are all the other teachers and students who share this classroom with Damon feeling any concern over the practice? "The box," which had been normalized, might not have become a point of contention without Rosa's perspective. That seems astounding to me. How and why did what were seemingly good intentions on the part of many end up with "the box" as an outcome? This is something I can never answer, but what I do know is that the questions sj Miller raises in her "Introduction" to this book are important ones: "And what would those spaces look like which would enable teachers to materialize those pedagogies and subjectivities? Collectively, can we move toward a space that we have yet to materialize such that teachers can practice and embody pedagogies that are unequivocally authentic?"

The word "collectively," in Miller's question, presents some of the challenges in this story. This series of events highlights how individuals partially position themselves based on their professional roles of the moment—teacher, cooperating teacher, student teacher, university supervisor, university professor, principal, and university department chair. Each of us had our own responsibilities, our roles, our closeness or distance to "the box" (which partially explains its meanings for us). But, there is more. It became clear during our discussion that personal experiences and belief systems also informed how each of us reacted.

As we attempted to talk through this situation, individuals' stories fostered fuller understanding of how professional and personal viewpoints shaped our individual readings of "the box." As we began our meeting, we decided that each of us should make a statement about the situation before determining next steps. Here are the layered stories that give my best recollection of what was said.

Judith starts: "The university is idealistic and doesn't teach prospective teachers how to deal with tough issues that just aren't solvable. I learned some starting points for curriculum in the program but not strategies for the complex situations that we find ourselves in. Who would ever imagine I would have this

Damon situation, and, a situation like this is more common than you'd imagine. Who would have guessed? But, the program should forecast and problem solve some of what we will face."

Judith's own story plays in here are well. She goes on to relate a story about a schoolmate when she was a child whom she believes had Downs syndrome. "There was a little room on one of the far ends of the school where several of these kids spent the day," Judith recalls. "This child would sometimes lapse into violent acts when he was frustrated." She describes the terror she felt in third grade when, on the way to school, she wouldn't give him her lunchbox. "I didn't feel like I was provoking him by saying 'no,' but he grabbed me around the throat. Just like that…out of the blue…of course, I'm not thinking Damon would do that, but you never know and I was just so frightened and a bigger kid wrestled him down and then when his father came to the school he was furious with me, asking why did I set him off. And I just thought then some kids just can't function in school. It isn't up to every other child to be fearful or put at risk or to feel responsible. I felt so bad. I cried right there and that made them think even more that it was my fault. I just learned to stay as far away as possible. And the next year, he really hurt another kid and he just disappeared from school. Okay, I don't like it but I was relieved. So maybe I am a little fearful of Damon and just don't feel I have the ways of helping him and I feel he is under control when he is feeling safe."

Rosa is next. "I hear what you are saying but pushing these kids away or letting them vanish, which is what it sounds like happened in your school, just isn't right. I just don't feel I can be part of all that. I spent my elementary years moving from school to school. My family worked the fields in Oregon, Washington, and Idaho and followed the crops. Only in the winter did we stay in any school more than a few weeks. I always felt like I was put in the last row, last desk and didn't have an identity or even a name. I was named the quiet migrant girl. In some ways I felt a bit like Damon. I never talked. I was never asked to talk or participate. I just did my work and my very bad English kept other students away from me. Sometimes two or three of us from migrant workers' families were in my class and that helped because I felt like that didn't set me apart so much. I just can't teach and do what teachers did to me."

For the life of me, I can't remember the name of the supervisor. She talked about other student teachers and the need to adjust to the classroom as it is set up. She did emphasize that Rosa needed to see herself as a visitor in the room and she asked what she thought the message of Rosa's actions might be to students. She talked about her own student teaching experience and how her co-operating teacher had always told her that the children needed to see them as the same person: "Have you thought that the children may see this as your criticism of their teacher? Or, they may think you are putting them in danger. They may not see what you are doing as noble or effective." She paused and hoped the questions and points she was making were sinking in. She wanted to change Rosa's mind. She talked a little more. "I think you can do what you want to do when this is your own class as long as you don't put the children in danger. The classroom is calm when Damon is in his box. Maybe you need to let it be or you need to decide that this is not a classroom where you can work." There, it was said. The agenda was now on the table.

Silences in Contested Spaces

Rosa starts to feel the sting in her eyes. The tears brim a few seconds later. She may have prepared herself for this, but she seems genuinely surprised and relieved: "You're right. I can't do this. I just can't. It isn't working when Damon is in the box or when he is out. I see that. I just can't do it."

In the end, Rosa decides not to return to this classroom. She wants to take some time away from teaching. She doesn't want us to find her another placement. I remember encouraging her to let this incident go and to move into a more productive teaching environment. Deep in my gut, I couldn't let this story go either. I knew it had much to teach me. I was not asked for my opinion by the university or the school. Others made the decisions, but I implicated myself by participating in the event and standing by silently as it reached resolution. I knew what wasn't right. A boy should not be in a box and a young teacher should not be boxed in to act on other people's beliefs. But, my way of handling the situation was to rage inside and remain silent.

From the perspectives of both explanatory and normative analysis, it seems almost incomprehensible that a sixth grade boy in a box in a classroom is a site for struggle. Just as absurd, however, are other contested spaces in schools that we could each name and are named in various ways in the essays collected in this book. As Anthony Giddens (1984) theorizes, "Space is not an empty dimension along which social groupings become structured, but has to be considered in terms of its involvement in the constitution of systems of interaction" (p. 368). In some uncommonsense ways, thinking about the box through systems of interaction—between school and university, between university and its graduate, between cooperating teacher and student teacher, between supervisor, faculty member, student teachers, and cooperating teacher and between teacher and student, between student teacher and student—makes visible institutional positions and interactions that often marginalize negotiations and create less than productive spaces. Conceptions of space that blur the binaries of private/public, oppositional/accountable, or open/closed may open dialogic sites/spaces that deterritorialize and reterritorialize competing social forces and determinations that attempt to "fix" meaning.

Margaret Kohn's (2003) point is apt here:

> Space affects how individuals and groups perceive their place in the order of things. Spatial configurations naturalize social relations by transforming contingent forms into a permanent landscape that appears as immutable rather than open to contestation. By providing a shared background, spatial forms serve the function of integrating individuals into a shared conception of reality. (pp. 3-4)

And Kohn goes on to point out that space can "initiate, maintain, or interrupt interaction" or "encourage or inhibit contact between people" (p. 155). The spatial configurations of "the box" in the classroom belie my understanding of how learning and teaching work in any of the dimensions of spaces that can be theorized.

The story of the box, then, is about a literal space. It is also about the constructed institutions and perspectives that theorize space as containment, boundary, border crossing, and as political and ideological. Much more than physical space is at stake here. Social practices occur within both physical and metaphoric spaces. The box created a structural regularity. That creation becomes normalized. So what is the relationship between physical space and social space? According to Andres Sayer (2000), physical space is a subset of social space rather than its opposite. It is the social space that has created the structural. The physical space is shaped and mediated by the social actors and subjects and is relative to the participants and the practices. It is our separate perceptions of that space that count because, in practice, there is value and symbolic importance (pp. 110-123). For example, if I say the box is "shutting out the possibility of interaction," that statement is relative to my understanding of the walls as impenetrable or impermeable. Or, if Damon perceives the walls as a safety, what projections and purposes can he make about the box as his space? So, our social practices incorporate physical space but these spaces carry divergent meanings. The point is: space carries meaning through the social practices that provide the interpretation of its meaning. In this case, when classroom space is restructured to hermetically seal or confine a student from the others, or, said differently, to give the student safe haven and space for safety, the verification of these points of view is only true in relation to how they matter to different people. It's actually possible that Damon thought of the box as a place rather than a space. The thought of the box as a space carries enormous ideological and symbolic value. If the box is a place, the meaning may be different. The box obviously has various and contested meanings. This takes us to the heart of the ethical and political implications of the box.

I understand, dear Readers, there is still indignation and concern that I am normalizing a box by objectifying it through this explanation. But "the box," literally and figuratively, exists in our pedagogies. On the one hand, schools are crowded places—competing intentions, values, and beliefs as well as the corporeal crowdedness. We segment, construct walls, erect barriers and security gates. We territorialize disciplines, label students, name tracks of performance, and objectify students through standards, grades, and tests. As I have also suggested, the use of space discloses how the ideo-politicization of social spaces carries ethical and normative implications. Our need to acknowledge and to think through the consequences of social spaces in schools may help us rethink their future constructions as exemplars of social justice. How might schools become spaces of heterogeneity that allow for contesting and contradictory and transdisciplinary understandings? What is the nature of the dialogic work that will be necessary to realize our goals? How do we acknowledge the grip of getting it right and come to terms that "right" has its own contingencies?

The Story Has an Ending but What Lingers On?

To the best of my knowledge, the students in Judith's class went on with their work and did not talk about Rosa's departure. Damon, well, he spent the rest of the year seemingly content in his box. Teachers, parents, students, and administrators did not talk about the box. It just was a part of classroom life that year. The supervisor supervised. Judith continued to engage students in amazing studies but didn't challenge them to study the situation in their own classroom. And, I continued to teach classes where we attempted to confront important issues, but I decided "the box" was too close to talk about when complex and difficult issues surfaced about competing intentions and tensions in classroom life. I learned through this incident that I did not know how to navigate or traverse all the streams of competing and conflicting values, beliefs, and purposes. I had much still to learn.

Damon's difficulties with social interaction, repetitive interests, and erratic responses to sensory experiences appear as classic symptoms of a spectrum disorder. Teachers have more information available today on autism than we did sixteen years ago. But, I am still not certain how or if teachers have the knowledge and strategies to work intensively with students who have particular challenges. Should teachers be equipped, or can they be equipped, to work with all students? The practices of inclusion are based on a social justice agenda. That agenda deserves more careful discussion and debate. Simply expecting that teachers can work productively with uniquely challenged students should be called into question.

How can we support teachers and ourselves as English educators when we sometimes lumber against an intransigent educational system, are implicated in the system in ways we don't fully understand, and are silent or silenced within the process? This story reminds me that it is often easier to design a curriculum to promote social justice than to develop pedagogies that materialize these beliefs in the buzz of daily classroom life and interactions. In this particular case, the school, the university, and the program struggled with how to enact social justice in teaching as well as in what was being taught.

If social justice pedagogy is about treating students equitably and fairly as well as teaching them to be fair and equitable with others, then what might we learn from the story of the box? How might this example help us understand the differences between curricula for social justice and the messages of social justice inherent in the classrooms, schools, and universities where we teach? In this particular case, what identities are constructed for and with Damon, the other students, the teacher, the student teacher, and others? And, what messages do students take away when we behave in ways that allow for reterritorialization and marginalization in a classroom? The unanswered questions and tensions tug and war with intentions and beliefs and outcomes.

Part of preparing teachers is to help them learn to negotiate ways to disrupt, critique, and challenge accepted practices and beliefs rather than simply trying to survive the school day or assuming that curriculum will engage students in social justice understandings and practices. We may find that it is possible and beneficial to learn about and talk about social justice in university classrooms, professional development seminars, and in what we read and write. But, when the actual school day begins, the pressures may overwhelm our best intentions and blur the theoretical lenses through which we engage with social justice, civic rights, difference, and equality.

Opening up dialogic spaces for ongoing contemplation, reflection, and dialogue is certainly helpful. In these spaces where we have the opportunity to stop the school day—university classrooms, seminars, workshops, or sitting in the wing-backed chair reading—we have time to reflect and rethink. But as the school day and year start again, we have students, colleagues, parents and all the interactions, the competing demands and expectations. In these moments, social justice considerations and agendas may be overwhelmed by the pragmatic.

As I have read the chapters in this book, I'm heartened that such spaces and moments are created which help us learn to examine the very different ways in which a social justice agenda is alive and flourishing in our English education programs. Part of our work as English educators is to help prospective teachers and they, their students, fight for the unpopular and the uncommonsensical—to help them learn to open the spaces that will allow them the opportunity to do the important work that needs to be done. This book offers example after example of the contexts and teaching life experiences that will engage, challenge, and encourage us to rethink what our most important responsibilities may be—along the lines of what is outlined in the Introduction as the 5 "Re-s."

As is the case for Rosa, a strong sense of justice made her vulnerable to institutional muscles that pushed for different actions and solutions, making it difficult for her to embody issues of social justice that were essential to her as teacher. What I've learned from this incident is that social injustices are often unrecognized and go unchallenged in schools because we convince ourselves we aren't contributing to the injustices if we are not direct participants or complicitous. Much work lies ahead. Resistances lurk in every dictate, standard, and developmental model. Social justice will not be achieved because we desire it or change what we do or design curriculum. We need to find ways to open the spaces wider, to make them more inviting and alluring. Every narrative in this book offers us another chance to look for the uncommonsense in the common. This collection calls us to enter a fourthspace where narratives of hopes and dreams and wide-awake purposes give us cause to pause and hope.

References

Giddens, A. (1984). *The Constitution of Society*. Cambridge: Polity Press.
Kohn, M. (2003). *Radical Space*. Ithaca: Cornell University Press.
Sayer, A. (2000). *Realism and Social Science*. London: Sage.

ACKNOWLEDGMENTS

The authors would like to thank the National Council of Teachers of English as well as the NCTE Commission on Social Justice for their unfailing support of social justice issues in the field of English education. We acknowledge sj for the theory of the loaded matrix and the new term "fourthspace," and for whose vision and dedication made this text possible. We would like to thank Ruth Vinz for her thoughtful and inspiring foreword. Her compelling story furthers our understanding of fourthspace and social justice. As she so poignantly says, "...narrative of hopes and dreams and wide-awake purposes give us cause to pause and hope." We are indebted to Don Zancanella for his inspiring endorsement and leadership in English education. We thank Sophie Appel, our production supervisor for her astute and kind assistance. Thanks also go to Gina Negley for her amazing graphic design talents. We make these personal acknowledgments:

David: I'd like to thank God and KENCA.

Laura: I want to thank Kristen and Stephanie for their willingness to share their stories. I also thank Ralph, Abigail, and Martha for their constant love and support.

Peggy: I would like to thank all educators/scholars who are committed to social justice teaching—especially those whose voices have challenged me, such as sj Miller, Carol Edelsky, and Wendy Kohli.

sj: I want to thank both Channell Wilson-Segura and Kristy Lorenzo for their courage as they continue their commitment to social justice teaching and blaze new territories in their schools. I thank Laura for stepping into the role as a wonderful and dedicated proof-reader and to my co-authors for their powerful, moving, and critical stories that have challenged me to push into fourthspace and continue my research therein.

We close with the infallible words of James Baldwin who reminds us to be indefatigable in our efforts to move forward in being socially just: "The paradox of education is precisely this—that as one begins to become conscious one begins to examine the society in which he [sic] is being educated."

sj Miller, Laura Bolf Beliveau, Todd DeStigter, David Kirkland, and Peggy Rice

1

Introduction
Fourthspace—Revisiting Social Justice in Teacher Education

sj Miller

Is concrete space becoming more difficult to inhabit as teachers claim that their subjectivities are in the middle of an ongoing tug-of-war between differing sociopolitical agendas? Are teachers entitled to more or less firstspace in their classrooms, which Soja (1996) refers to as the real and concrete spaces that humans inhabit? Or, are teachers inhabiting a space and time where they must pool their resources to even imagine what is left of our concrete school spaces? Collectively, can we move toward a space that we have yet to materialize such that teachers can practice and embody pedagogies that are unequivocally authentic? And what would those spaces look like which would enable teachers to materialize those pedagogies and subjectivities?

Such questions beget a deeper concern for us about how teachers can embody a social justice pedagogy and identity when school districts where they teach may not, and are forced to go "into the closet" because their beliefs are not supported by their firstspace environment. On the other hand, when teachers are supported teaching a social justice pedagogy, what is different about those teachers and how are they supported in their efforts? At the university level, we are concerned about how to ensure that a social justice agenda that we each embody has efficacy in schools and over time especially when the language of national accreditation standards such as with National Council for Accreditation of Teacher Education (NCATE) has shifted away from using social justice because of its inherent politicized nature (according to the Religious Right). We question how we can sustain our efforts if the spaces we inhabit are becoming more minimal and less visible. This means that we must reconsider how we are approaching social justice pedagogy in our university spaces and how we can best stabilize preservice teacher identity over space and time.

When we speak about social justice pedagogy, we mean that we believe that all students, regardless of their differences, should be treated fairly and equitably in schools. This also means that we deconstruct and critique the ways that curriculum is socially constructed and consider the foundations of its origins. We apply such considerations to our classrooms and in our praxis. We are relentless in our efforts to meet students where they are in their lives and meet them where they are in their efforts. This means, students are not to blame for perceived shortcomings, rather we look at them within a matrix of issues that may impact their ability to live up to their potentials. We liken our sense of social justice to that of Miller and Norris (2007) reflect on what social justice means to them:

> We have come to embody social justice as a lifestyle that marries body, mind, and soul or the beliefs married to the actions that lead to an intrapersonal level of awareness. It can mean a lifestyle that is committed to the belief that all people are entitled to the same core basic tenets as stated in the Constitution of the United States: life, liberty, and the pursuit of happiness. As such, each person is entitled to the same opportunities regardless of background or acquired privilege. It means standing up for injustice and discrimination in all forms with regard to: race, ethnicity, gender, gender expression, age, appearance, ability, national origin, religion, weight, height, sexual orientation, social class, environment, ecology, culture, spiritual and animal. For us social justice is not something we just do or enact in the classroom to meet NCATE's (National Council for Accreditation of Teacher Education) or NCTE's (National Council of Teachers of English) standards rather it is quite the opposite; for social justice is in our lifestyles and exists on many levels and takes on many shapes and forms. This means that we are conscious about what we eat, where we shop, how we spend our money, what causes we give to, how we become allies for others, what we read, and how we, not if we, stand up in situations that require a voice or an advocate. For us standing up no longer becomes a choice; rather it is core to our commitment to social justice and social change. By embodying such a lifestyle, social justice travels through our teaching and impacts our curricular choices, texts, pedagogies, and our professional relationships. We feel that living a life that aligns body, mind, and soul strengthens our core selves and builds emotional and spiritual integrity. Most important to us is that we have to be able to understand and appreciate all of our students, especially those who we perceive are different from how we perceive ourselves, so that we can instruct and facilitate fairly and equitably. (pp. 3-4)

Teachers teach in pre-assigned classroom spaces, social spaces which are highly politicized (albeit mostly unseen) as competing national and local agendas vie for ownership over curriculum and textbooks. Varying political ideologies and hidden agendas of private constituents and government decisions greatly constrain teachers and instructors in teacher education programs to adopt their beliefs (Apple, 2002). Social spaces are formed for all kinds of reasons but are often constructed out of necessity and are impacted by political (power) and social ideologies (Foucault 1980, 1986; Lefebvre 1991). Foucault (1986) and

Bourdieu (1980) suggest that the effects of power construct identities, and that the embodiment of identities in spaces is vulnerable as a result of power. Thus, the identity of the teacher becomes a tug-of-war on the mind and body in which the individual is being co-constructed by factors well beyond the individual's control.

Some teachers capitulate when they sense that they are powerless to affect change. This makes us consider how can we in English education support teachers whose social justice pedagogy becomes part of their embodied vulnerability? Bullough (1987) noted that "many of the teachers who remain in classrooms end up teaching in ways that are inconsistent and even contradictory to their initial pedagogical beliefs, goals, and expectations" (quoted in Rogers & Babinski, 2002, p. 3). Of great concern to Bullough (1987) is that teachers often fall back on the more traditional paradigms of teaching that they were instructed to use when they experience a dissonance between university teaching and classroom space. Therefore, it is critical that we open up conversations during students' liminal time in teacher preparation courses so that we can support their emotional, cognitive, and corporeal development as social justice educators so that they have the tools that they can draw from in case they should experience duress. How can we do good work that has long-standing efficacy unless we help build and strengthen the emotional, cognitive, and corporeal muscles that teachers take with them into their teaching placements?

Background to Our Work

Several recent works have explored ways in which teachers affect an agenda of social justice in their classroom practices (Cochran-Smith, 2004; Howard, 2006; Ladson-Billings & Tate, 2006; Miller & Norris, 2007). However, what research in English education has not yet documented is how preservice and inservice English teachers negotiate the transfer of social justice pedagogies they learn in university methods classes to their own work as beginning full-time teachers. That is to say, English education researchers have not yet shown precisely how preservice and inservice English teachers—as they move from universities to their own classrooms—interpret, respond to, and embody social justice theories in their classroom practices (Garmon, 2004; Ladson-Billings, 2005; Leland & Harste, 2005). Based on a set of teacher narratives, we offer a critical and evidenced-based view of English teachers' interpretations of, responses to, and embodiments of social justice as they move beyond the university and into their own classrooms. These narratives explore the complex shifts and concessions that English teachers often make when transitioning between preservice and inservice spaces—shifts which allow teachers to embrace and negotiate a social justice agenda in their classrooms, or for some, to modify, or even abandon it altogether. We believe that documenting and disseminating these narratives is important because such stories have strong potential to foster English educators' commitments to social justice teaching and to demonstrate how such commitments can be put into practice.

Our book comes out of a set of conversations that took place during a meeting of the Conference on English Education (CEE) Commission on Social Justice at the National Council of Teacher of English (NCTE) 2006 Annual Meeting in Nashville, TN. The Commission identified important goals related to identifying the connections between social justice theories in English education and social justice teaching in English/language arts (ELA) classrooms. The primary goal of the Commission's efforts has been to offer research/narratives that explore the nature of social justice teaching in English teacher education and its application to English classrooms and make meaning of its implications for English teachers and their classrooms so that university instructors can reflect on and strive to create the conditions necessary that can foster and affirm preservice concerns around enacting social justice teaching. In other words, how can we know that that social justice teaching has an impact over space and time? Some of the commission members have come together in this collective to share narratives of their own awakening into social justice teaching.

Based upon the Commission's larger aims, the book has two interrelated goals. *Narratives of Social Justice Teaching* provides portraits of English teachers, including university instructors, their current preservice teachers and former preservice but now inservice teachers, documenting the ways in which they have transferred what they learned about social justice teaching in their university methods classes to their own secondary and elementary school classrooms. It also examines how these spaces shape teachers' entry into social justice teaching by offering a fresh perspective on the specific, context-dependent pathways and mechanisms through which English teachers enter school culture and respond to their own racial, sexual, and financial positions in relation to the gendered, raced, and classed positions of their schools, students, and classrooms. Through our writings, we honor and pay homage to the trailblazing work of those leaders, activists, scholars, teachers, and students who have cut down the forest before we even ventured into such territory. In this light, we continue their tradition.

Studying Particular Teacher Narrative: Toward a Theory of Practice

Narratives of Social Justice Teaching has grown out of a concern to understand what is retained (and what may be lost) in translation between preservice and inservice teaching experiences—and why. What happens when English teacher educators embody and support progressive language and literacy pedagogies in climates where practicing English teachers bump up against institutional barriers during their inservice and preservice teaching placements? According to

Duncan-Andrade (2004), many teachers often feel under-supported, and many more abandon their social justice agenda, opting for less controversial and less efficacious pedagogical options. This is of further concern because teachers who adopt a social justice pedagogy may also become targets by ideologues who do not advocate for a balanced curriculum (see "David Horowitz Freedom Center").

The core of this work responds to a timely need to link teacher education to a social justice agenda that challenge dominant ideologies through the pedagogies and practices to which we ascribe through our teaching. The book explores a theory of practice: how social justice theories are enacted as social justice practices. To this end, Cochran-Smith (2004) suggests that for teacher education to move toward a social justice agenda it must be conceptualized as both "a learning problem and a political problem" (p. 2). Our research responds to Cochran-Smith's call to link research to practice and to the "contexts and participants in teacher education" (Cochran-Smith & Zeichner, 2005). More specifically, it raises questions about research and practice with relation to the "instructional strategies and texts" that our programs use and the "unexplored topics related to teacher preparation," as these relate to how preservice teachers' "beliefs, attitudes, skills and practices" impact their students' learning opportunities and attitudes.

In effect, English teachers narrate stories, often previously untold, about the tensions between social justice theories and social justice teachings. Their stories can offer access to a set of negotiations that might help teacher educators better understand ways to prepare English teachers to put social justice theories into practice. Both preservice and inservice English teachers can draw from particular narratives to develop "familiar forms of agency" (Dyson, 2003) for engaging in meaningful action and to construct a functional understanding around practicing social justice teaching. In this book, we follow the narrative relationships of teachers who weave themselves in and out of conceptual places in order to stitch together practices that allow them to teach for social justice in a particular setting.

Rationale for Narratives

Through *Narratives of Social Justice Teaching*, we aim to document specifically the range of ways in which social justice agendas are put into practice in schools. We aim as well, to use the vantage point of classroom teachers to articulate a vision of English teacher education that moves beyond the traditionally tidy developmental path of theory divorced from practice. This "neat" path has persisted even as theoretical explanations for teacher development have multiplied—explanations that include linear, behavioristic lists of singular skills, developmental "stages" predicting carefully sequenced behaviors, and apprenticeship models tracing singular practices (e.g., "accommodating," "negotiating," and "resisting"). This "neat" developmental model, we contend, is inattentive to practicing teachers' complex juxtapositions, blendings, and differentiations of practices from an array of sources. In other words, these developmental models do not sufficiently account for the specific social, cultural and pedagogical contexts of beginning teachers' attempts to affect a social justice agenda.

The developmental vision put forward in this book builds, in part, on our own past efforts as both English teachers and English teacher educators. Those efforts have been driven by a desire to contribute to a view of English teacher development that is not predicated on the existence of a theory/practice divide. The books based on research projects have been attempts to broaden the view of the negotiation involved in English teacher development in school contexts: the ways in which social justice teaching is intertwined with diverse experiences in classrooms; with engagement in peer relationships; in relation to school curriculum pressures; and, potentially, with critical engagement with the dominant ideologies of what it means to teach English. Unlike other texts, this book aims to detail the specific developmental mechanisms—the recontextualization processes—through which English teachers' experiences in classrooms organize their teaching practice. This is not to say that preservice instruction does not matter. It simply suggests that we are currently unclear as to what is passed on between preservice and inservice spaces which, in addition to other issues, the proposed book explicitly explores. Instruction is informed by researchers who construct teacher learning contexts beyond the preservice phase, and is focused on English teachers collective learning experiences between preservice and inservice spaces, which inform their agency and efficacy in teaching practice.

Negotiating Social Justice Theory into Practice

Teachers must negotiate their own belief systems when they are teaching students all of the time, but how can teachers stay true to themselves while they truly have no ownership in their school spaces? Since schools are competing sites for political agendas, we must reconsider ways to support teachers who embrace a social justice pedagogy. This question warrants a discussion about a ways to consider the struggle between personal and political space. One way to reconsider this is to first recognize that horizontal space is claimed by stakeholders and by moving toward a vertical space, or space that cannot be seen to the visible eye, vertical space can become a haven for how to support preservice teachers in their conceptualization of social justice pedagogy. I will refer to vertical space as fourthspace, where we build on the concepts introduced by Soja (1996) of firstspace (concrete space), secondspace (or imagined space), and thirdspace (real and imagined space). Fourthspace becomes a space that is conceptualized by a double helix, a three-dimensional twisted shape like a spring, screw, or spiral:

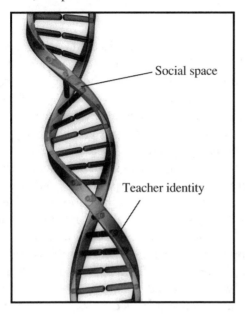

Figure 1. This is an example of teacher identity as stabilized in fourthspace. The right arm of the helix is considered the social space while the left arm of the helix is the teacher identity.

The coiled structure of the double helix is linked by hydrogen bonds that form a spiral configuration, with the two strands along the same axis that are oriented in opposite directions. A single helix would only be one arm of the double helix, say for example the left or right arm. Each helix, traveling in opposite directions, reflects an emotional, corporeal, and cognitive shift of a teacher as s/he relocates from the firstspace classroom, to a vertical space. This vertical relocation is a site for teachers to do the 5 "re-s": reflect, reconsider, reconceptualize, rejuvenate and to reengage. I suggest that this fourthspace help them resist against a psychasthenic (Olalquiaga, 1992, as in Soja, 1996) state, that is, a state in which we are unable to demarcate our own personal boundaries and become engulfed by and camouflage ourselves in the scholastic milieu. The 5 "re-," as conceptualized by fourthspace, can bring teachers into a different level of awareness about their praxis.

If we reonceptualize teacher identity as fluid (Miller & Norris, 2007), we open up the possibilities that as an individual morphs and appropriates different qualities of selfhood into his/her teacher identity, we can imagine that the teacher's identity can impact a space just as a space can impact a teacher's identity.

Building on the importance of being self-actualized and self-realized from Palmer (1998) and hooks (1994), Alsup (2006) in *Teacher Identity Discourse*s found that only the teachers who had a strong sense of how their personal identity (dis)connected to their professional identity were able to successfully transition into teaching. Those who experienced an identity crisis were more likely to leave. We must strive to help teachers know themselves in a variety of times and spaces and help them determine what are the best strategies they can employ in each context. Bloom (1998) refers to this as nonunitary subjectivities.

Alsup (2006) suggests that to develop a critical pedagogy, teacher education must consider how the individual comes to terms with a professional identity. A critical pedagogy seeks to challenge how unequal social relations manifest in people's experiences. Critical pedagogy is embodied when body and mind are united and people are more prepared to challenge social relations and barriers that may seek to dis-integrate body from mind (Hocking, Haskell, & Linds, 2001; Miller & Norris, 2007). When body and mind are united, transformation begins. Teaching is more than an intellectual act, it involves how teachers "move, laugh, dramatize, perform, smile, point, sigh, joke, gesticulate, write, and move around the room as necessary, and we want them thinking through each of these transitions and we want our teachers to be aware of their feelings, thoughts, and emotions as they respond in kind and thoughtful ways to students (Miller & Norris, 2007, pp. 15-16). Helping teachers cultivate both their corporeal responses to social justice can help them more fully understand their own professional identity development because "to ignore the mind's relationship to the body in preservice methods is to further political ideologies that serve to perpetuate divisive hierarchies and feed patriarchy in our democracy"(Miller & Norris, 2007, p. 16). A brief background on emotional and corporeal responses can help us understand how the double helix can serve as means to support teachers in affirming a social justice pedagogy and identity.

Teacher Emotion

Teachers are not immune from having emotional responses to issues in school. In fact, teaching is a highly emotional profession laden with the ups and downs of professional and student achievement often predicated on factors far beyond any teacher's control. Are teachers expected to maintain a mask that hides their true feelings and act as a mannequin sans emotion? Research on teacher emotion can be dichotomized into two waves. During the first wave, research on teacher emotion was viewed as purely a cognitive activity (Lupton,

1998). During the second wave over the last two decades, there has been increased focus of the role emotion plays in teaching as focused through social relationships within the school context (Acker, 1992, 1999; Golby, 1996; Hargreaves, 1998, 2000, 2001; Kelchtermans, 1999; Nias, 1989, 1993, 1996; Schmidt, 2000). Kemper (1978), sees emotion as "a relatively short-term evaluative response essentially positive or negative involving distinct somatic (and often cognitive) components" (p. 47). Lazarus (1999) contributes that emotions "refer to a complex organized system consisting of thoughts, beliefs, motives, meanings, subjective bodily experiences, and physiological states (as in Van-Veen & Sleegers, 2006, p. 88). More importantly according to Lazarus, is that the processes these emotions elicit are motivational, relational, and cognitive (Lazarus, 1991). These studies suggest that the social environment combined with personality and one's motivations affect the emotional response of the person to a given situation.

Gerth and Mills (1953) suggest that the individual's emotions and the institutions (social spaces) they inhabit and the roles they have therein are inexorably linked. Armon-Jones (1986) concurs and says that the emotions that individuals use reflect the roles and purpose they serve in an institution. Institutions tend to both privilege and "value rationality and dispassionate discourse and in effect, marginalize the free expression of emotion" (Ferguson, 1984 as in Winograd, 2003, p. 1645). Teachers are therefore vulnerable to assuming the emotional responses that the institution embodies while forsaking their own. Hochschild (1983) refers to this as emotional labor, which is the process of "inhibiting, generating, or displaying" an emotion to elicit an emotional response in someone else. How can we therefore affirm a teacher's real emotion if s/he is pressured to conform? In fact, studies in social psychology and sociology of emotions show the importance of self-expression to the health of the individual as a way to relate and communicate beliefs (Armon-Jones, 1986; Goffman, 1959; Hochschild, 1983; Kemper, 1978). If teachers must "closet" their feelings, then we are constructing disembodied teachers.

Jaggar's (1989) feminist perspective on *outlaw emotions* is important to explore here. She maintains that emotion is linked to power and states:

> Outlaw emotions may provide the first indications that something is wrong with the way alleged facts have been construed, with accepted understandings of how things are.... Only when we reflect on our initial puzzling, irritability, revulsion, anger, or fear may we bring to consciousness our "gut level" awareness that we are in a situation of coercion, cruelty, injustice or danger. (Jaggar, p. 161, as in Winograd, 2003, p. 1644)

Jaggar sustains this by suggesting that when we name our emotions it can lead to change because it can provoke initiatives to alter unjust contexts. Zembylas (2003) brings these issues to a head when he suggests that sociopolitical issues and cultural aspects undergird the emotions of the teacher. An approach to help unpack teachers' emotions and a way to help teachers emote might be to ask preservice teachers to bring in their outlaw emotions and spend time unpacking them within the context of the university. When done in a collective, more voices and solidarity can both inspire and motivate collective change. In fact, Zembylas (2003) suggests that "teachers' emotions can become sites of resistance and self-(trans)formation" (p. 106).

Corporeal Responses

When we speak about corporeal responses, we mean how the teacher's body responds emotionally to issues. The theory of emotional contagion "suggests that all participants in communicative exchange are susceptible to each other's emotions and the contagion effect" (Hatfield, Cacioppo, & Rapson, 1994; Mottet & Beebe, 2000). As such, emotions tend to influence behavior, or bodily responses (Cacioppo & Gardner, 1999; Russell & Mehrabian, 1978). Mehrabian (1981) suggests that expression that involves nonverbal messages affects others' emotional responses and behavior. Further, Mehrabian's (1971) research shows that teachers who are immediate with forward body leans, direct eye contact, and intentional gestures tend to be viewed as likable and approachable. In response, students' nonverbal responses reflected a teacher's positive perceptions of teaching effectiveness and satisfaction and reflected how students felt about the course and the instructor. Hargreaves's (1998, 2000, 2001) findings based on the work of Hochschild's (1983) "emotional labor" reveal "that the relationship of teacher to student "energized and articulated everything these teachers did: including how they taught, how they planned, and structures in which they teach" (p. 111). Such findings indicate that the emotional relationship of teacher to student has great bearing upon the emotional experience of the teacher in the classroom.

An outcome for our discipline is that instructors should be proactive about how to engender emotional contagion in such a fashion that the classroom can be a site where individuals are not devoid of emotion but that the expression of self can become a transformative tool toward a more democratic space in schools. In other words, our emotions are heavily tied to our bodies and our cognitive processes. As a way to help reconsider teachers' emotions and corporeal responses, we put forth the 5 "re-s": reflect, reconsider, reconceptualize, rejuvenate and reengage. By no means are the 5 "re-s" a sure-fired way of helping students remain in teaching but it becomes an immediate strategy that can empower them to think through and reconsider difficult issues. By taking students through the 5 "re-s" and then by understanding and embodying the step-by-step process, students develop critical tools that they can reflect on when they are faced with difficult decisions.

The 5 "Re-s"

Most of us have had moments when a student asks us a question, challenges us on a position, or pushes in a direction when we don't know how to respond. Some of us are good fakers and can respond with intelligent feedback and others may feign an answer in order to save face. By conceptualizing the 5 "re-s" in fourthspace, teachers will be able to transcend the horizontal space and engage in a quick "check out" or a "critical second" that may go undetected by the audience. Such a check out, we suggest, is imperative so that a teacher can quickly reflect, reconsider, reconceptualize, rejuvenate and reengage in a manner of seconds. As we develop these skills with students, they will be able to move from a potentially destabilizing moment into a restabilizing stance and articulate a response to the best of their ability. Such movement, albeit unseen to the audience, is a strategy to preserve and enhance social justice and other kinds of teaching in the classroom.

Reflect

As we work with our teachers in our university spaces, and in our supervisory roles, it is critical that we open up the channels of discourse that provide ample opportunity for them to reflect on what it means to be a social justice educator. We must also help them understand that some of the districts where they teach may not support a social justice classroom or a teacher who teaches outside of prescriptive expectations. Reflection can lead to change and by engaging teachers in such opportunities we can help them on their way to social justice teaching; even when they may be far away from the safety of our classrooms. Reflection can take many different forms and we provide you with some suggestions for how to foster reflection. Ask students to:

- Script what social justice means.
- Describe their belief systems and how they came to terms with them.
- Craft their pedagogies and share them aloud while inviting feedback.
- Describe the instances where they have summoned their beliefs about social justice.
- Describe instances when they have enacted, embodied, and/or been an ally for social justice.
- Reflect on what is unjust around them in society, schools, and families.
- Describe what a social justice classroom would look like.
- Role play scenes that involve something unjust, i.e., discrimination or bullying in school based on actual or perceived looks, social class, age, sexual orientation, ability, national origin, language, ethnicity, against someone, and then describe how to problem solve the situation.

- Consider a time when they have been oppressed, how would they have handled it differently today?
- Bring in actual scenarios that happened in the field and discuss them in class. Ask for feedback and develop a strategy to reengage.
- Research organizations that are in the community, state, or nation that support different issues, write them, gather information.
- Build a resource pool of like-minded friends, teachers, and community members and meet once a month about social justice issues.
- Research a school site and conduct a survey about the campus climate. Then consider how to enact change.

We believe that teachers, who embody tools, are teachers who can act with confidence in situations that may be more sensitive.

Reconsider

After teachers have time to reflect, they enter the stage to reconsider what transpired or what could possibly transpire. Opening up spaces in our classrooms that allow teachers and students to reconsider what they did and how they might do something differently, engages them in the opportunity of praxis. Most of us benefit from reconsidering how we conduct situations and by offering feedback we can create critical moments that can empower teachers to reengage with a cadre of tools and strategies. Ask students to:

- Bring in stories from the field related to social justice and ask the class how they might have responded differently to the situation. Then ask the student to write on what s/he gained from the session.
- Research some aspect of an issue they dealt with or deal with in the field, and ask them to discover something new about the topic.
- Review the First Amendment and ask them how it is/isn't and can't be embodied fully in schools. Ask them to reconsider how to address certain social justice issues when First Amendment rights are suspended while in schools.
- Research discrimination policies in the school district and state where they teach and then help them make informed decisions about whether or not they can or should teach in that district or state.
- Reconsider what it means to be a social justice teacher in a school district that doesn't support teaching for social change.
- Identify how an issue that is important to them ties into a national issue and then reconsider how they might be proactive about it in their schools.

Reconceptualize

As students move into this phase, they can begin to shift their thinking in ways that are more aligned with their belief systems. Moving into this stage, students develop a sense that there is more than one way to handle an issue around social justice when it emerges. Reconceptualization as a tool can lead students to become visionaries of hope who are empowered to not only create change in their classrooms, but also in their students' lives, their own communities and possibly even at the state or national level. When reconceptualizing, ask students to:

- Diagram or map out the school and look at its organizations. Ask them to reconsider how the school could be designed differently so that it would be to the betterment of the student body and faculty.
- Consider what other clubs the schools they work in might need and then do the research to begin that club.
- Meet with other like-minded teachers and identify gaps in instruction related to social justice and then develop a plan that can be strategically mapped out and implemented over time.
- Revisit the curriculum and reflect on what community links can be made to the school.
- Revisit what it means to be a social justice educator and align it to what is or isn't being enacted in their schools, then reflect on how they can become more involved.
- Imagine how their own classroom students can take on more of a leadership role in their own schools and then create a focus group with students and identify what is missing from the school (clubs, safe spaces, policies, etc).
- Identify an idea they want to reconceptualize related to social justice, prepare a presentation for class, and then open it up for discussion and feedback.

Rejuvenate

Teachers who engage in social justice work may feel a sense of isolation and marginalization if their beliefs are ignored or they are labeled as trouble-makers. Such teachers may experience burnout, abandon their social justice agenda or may even leave teaching altogether. Since teachers who embrace social justice pedagogy may become targets in their own schools, we must consider ways to support them in their efforts by affording them possibilities to rejuvenate their spirits. When working with students to help them rejuvenate, ask students to:

- Form and create ally groups where they can go to for support.
- Consider ways they can regroup after tough days teaching (exercise, massage, candles, movies, reading, TV, dinner, walking, talking, etc.).
- Identify a mentor with whom they can process.
- Create a plan for taking days off. What would that look like? How do you know when its time to take time off?
- Discuss personal symptoms of burnout and create a contingency plan when it begins.
- Look inward and try to identify root causes of frustration. Identify triggers and be aware of what causes them.
- Remember that stress can be part of the teaching profession and that they need to develop healthy detachment from situations where they may have little or if any control.
- Remember that they cannot be super-heroes but they can make a   significant difference in what they do on a daily basis (even though it may not immediately be self-evident).

Reengage

As we enter the last stage of the 5 "re-s," it's necessary to remind ourselves that some students may leave the profession when they come to see how difficult it can be to affect systemic change. Though this is a reality that faces our profession, we need to consider non-incendiary ways to support teachers in their efforts to not only stay engaged in a system that may not be socially justice-minded but also how to reengage with a system that may not support their belief systems. How can we support inchoate teachers in their social justice development while also preparing them for some of the pitfalls they may encounter? We can:

- Be honest about the spaces that have more inclusive teaching environments and support teachers in going after what they desire.
- Help students consider the pros and cons of teaching and help them see the bigger picture of their lives.
- Offer them curricular and social support that might help sustain them when times are tough.
- Form heterotopias, which are a "real" place where there is a "sort of mixed, joint experience" or a "counter-site" occupied and created by those who contest the dominant sites (Foucault, 1986, p. 24), so that teachers can refer to the skills that they have learned to embody as a tool of resistance against larger and more dangerous sociopolitical agendas.

- Encourage them to move into higher education after some time after they have spent at least three years teaching (since that is a minimum qualification for most university positions in English education.
- Remind them to reflect on what is important to them about teaching and support them in how they can be their best in their schools.
- Encourage them to join national organizations, attend conferences, and present research with the National Council Teachers of English, International Reading Association, American Educational Research Association, or the Shepard Symposium on Social Justice.
- Encourage them to subscribe to national journals in their field like the *English Journal, English Education, Journal of Adolescent and Adult Literacy, Reading Research Quarterly, Social Justice, Teaching Tolerance,* and *Teacher's College Press.*
- Invite them to create community links to their classrooms so they be gin to develop a larger networking community.
- Invite them to revisit and revise their personal pedagogies from time to time.

In summation, as teachers develop the skills to work through the five stages, they can begin to enact fourthspace when they are in firstspace teaching and restabilize without walking out of the class. Such skills will enable them to think through difficult issues, tap into past experiences to retain perspective, and respond with dignity.

Format for the Chapters

In order to write this book, we have invited both preservice and inservice teachers to collaborate on chapters. Their narratives, in particular the ones that identify their teaching successes, barriers, gaps, and the dissonances between university teaching and classroom practice, are vital to this book. Their voices along with our input demonstrate ways that English teachers can came to terms with our own stances toward social justice despite pressures from outside as we reflect with them on how they negotiate and navigate social justice teaching in their own classrooms. They comment upon how our experiences impact our teaching and translate into classroom practice. We hope that by highlighting the localized, contextualized stories of beginning teachers as they tell them, we as English educators will learn much about how we might reconstitute our methods coursework to prepare our students to negotiate this transfer effectively.

Each chapter will have a similar choreography. Through the narratives, we (along with preservice and inservice teacher participants) will each reflect upon how we have come to terms with our own stances toward social justice. Each chapter will, therefore, explore how negotiating the tensions between theory and practice have impacted our social justice teaching. The chapters will also explore how this process of negotiation translates into effective classroom practice. Through our stories, we offer units about social justice teaching framed by teachers' pedagogical stances that illustrate how they have interpreted university-based teaching about social justice theory and actualized it in the context of their classrooms. Each team of writers decided upon the format that worked best for them and so we have formatted chapters that are conceptualized differently. We chose to let the format develop authentically based on each group as a collective. Although we each wrote with our self-selected pre- and inservice teacher by different means, we did begin with a common set of questions.

For ourselves we asked:
- When did I first become aware of my own social justice pedagogy? Events? Class? Speakers? Personal experiences, etc.? Why is that important to you?
- How is social justice entwined in my pedagogy? Life?
- How do I help English education students develop a critically conscious social justice pedagogy?
- What are my concerns about its efficacy in the schools?

For our preservice teachers we asked:
- When did you first become aware of your own social justice pedagogy? Events? Class? Speakers? Personal experiences, etc.? Why is that important to you?
- How is social justice entwined in your pedagogy? Life?
- How do you help classroom students develop a critically conscious social justice stance?
- What are the tensions, barriers that affect this?
- Describe your most rewarding experience enacting social justice pedagogy in the classroom.

For our inservice teachers we asked:
- When did you first become aware of your own social justice pedagogy? Events? Class? Speakers? Personal experiences, etc?
- Why is that important to you?
- How is social justice entwined in your pedagogy? Life?
- How do your help classroom students develop a critically conscious social justice stance?
- What are the tensions, barriers that affect this?
- Describe your most rewarding experience enacting social justice pedagogy in the classroom.

- Describe if you are still embracing social justice teaching in your classroom. If not, tell me why.

Chapters 2-5 were each co-authored by a university professor in English education, one of their current preservice teachers and a current inservice teacher. For Chapter 2, "It's in the Telling and the Sharing: Becoming Conscious of Social Justice through Communal Exploration," Laura, Kristen, and Stephanie discuss their definitions of social justice and commitment to infusing curriculum with social justice issues from middle school and high school perspectives. They also discuss how their privileged backgrounds play into the mix. Their chapter is organized as a dialogue of equal voices that integrates personal narratives to illustrate their ideas. Chapter 3, "Quiet Tensions in Meaning: A Conversation with a "Social Justice" Teacher," reveals the story of a teacher, Danielle, as she struggles to define justice as a high school English teacher. From her struggle, David and she seek to understand how social justice gains meaning, especially at points of incongruence, between preservice and inservice teaching spaces. In doing so, they address two questions: what does it mean to teach for justice, and how does a teacher know? These questions of meaning, they suggest, calls for constant conversation—internal and external dialogue—about the tensions in words and a willingness to revise the meanings of words to accommodate the pragmatics of actual teaching situations. Further, they suggest that the voyage from preservice to inservice teaching spaces is one complicated by this tension, in part, due to the uncertainty masked in meanings, collisions of interests attached to words, and the ever-shifting tilt in their understandings of why they teach, be it for social justice or social ill. In Chapter 4, "Dream Big: The Power of Literature, Imagination, and the Arts," Peggy, Alena, Jamey, and Emily Marie reflect on their commitment to teaching for social justice with an emphasis on developing community and incorporating literature reflecting diverse perspectives with the arts to create spaces for developing understandings. They also explore the value of the 5 "re-s" in fourthspace. In chapter 5, "Multicultural Spaces Meet Rural Places," sj, Channell, and Kristi reflect on how they each came to term with their desires to be social justice-minded educators in different contexts (both middle school and high school teaching) and during different times. As a collective, they discovered that what was significant to the development and embodiment of their social justice consciousnesses was that they were affirmed in their teacher education programs. They recognized that the stabilization of their social justice identities became a safety net of empowerment from which they could draw from when they faced adversity in their school spaces. In chapter 6, "Lifting the Veil of Ignorance: Thoughts on the Future of Social Justice Teaching," Todd DeStigter draws the book to a close as he tells the story of his work with a student at an alternative Chicago high school, and through this story (and Melville's "Bartleby the Scrivener") raises what he thinks are important questions that suggest some needed revisions within the current paradigm of social justice teaching. His chapter calls for new ways of thinking about teaching for social justice in the future.

Conclusion

We are not aware of any other publication aimed to situate a developmental study of teachers within narratives of particular teacher experiences negotiating social justice theory and practice between preservice and inservice spaces. Those interested in contemporary teacher education between intentions and practice usually focus on traditional, less progressive forms of teaching. They fear that a social justice view of teaching may reduce teachers' actual lives to a description of dogmatic/didactic teaching. But this book's vision is predicated on the interplay between theory and practices, on the stories that teachers take away from negotiating preservice and inservice spaces. Moreover, the luminaries of these narratives, the teachers, are not so easily reduced. We think readers will enjoy coming to know them.

To our knowledge, no book has featured the collaborative braiding of university, inservice, and preservice teachers' voices exclusively on social justice teaching. We hope to begin the discussion about the efficacy of social teaching and pedagogy and how its enactment may bump up against institutional barriers once teachers are inservice. We hope that our text will help our field reconsider the kinds of issues and pedagogical approaches that we use so that we can begin to reflect on how we can better serve our inchoate teachers on issues related to social justice teaching.

Although there are studies on how emotions are triggered and how teachers deflect them, our field would greatly benefit from more studies conducted on emotional teacher contagion (Mottet & Beebe, 2000) especially within the social-psychological cognitivist or appraisal theory fields (VanVeen & Sleegers, 2006) which focuses on how context produces and shapes different emotions. Also needed, are more studies on how political and cultural issues, as Zembylas (2003) suggests "regulate emotional rules and require emotion management in the context of curriculum and teaching" (p. 113). We do need to rise above antiquated paradigms that privileges certain emotions and behaviors over others and therefore must be kept out of the classroom. Perhaps, we need to have conversations that challenge patriarchal beliefs around gendered expressions and dominant perceptions about what expression of feeling means. Postmodern perceptions of emotion would elicit the significance of the presence of emotion in the classroom which can be polemicized against the manufacturing of teachers for reproduction of knowledge (Apple, 2002).

Perhaps we should embrace the idea of the *via negativa* introduced by Emmanuel Levinas, as the unknowing, which is the concept that unknowability can play an important role in teaching and learning. In this place of unknowing, individuals have time to reflect on pedagogy and come to terms with the revelation that unknowing can lead to great outcomes with unpredictable possibilities. In this way we can support both veteran and preservice teachers alike by affirming their social justice stances emotionally and corporeally when situational demands and educational reforms are tugging at their seams.

References

Acker, S. (1992). Creating careers: Women teachers at work. *Curriculum Inquiry, 22,* 141-163.

———. (1999). *The realities of teachers' work: Never a dull moment.* London: Cassell.

Alsup, J. (2006). *Teacher identity discourses: Negotiating personal and professional spaces.* Mahwah: Lawrence Erlbaum.

Apple, M. (2002). *Official knowledge.* New York: Routledge.

Armon-Jones, C. (1986). The social functions of emotions. In R. Harre (Ed.), *The social construction of emotions* (pp. 57-82). Oxford: Basil Blackwell.

Bloom, L.R. (1998). *Under the sign of hope: Feminist methodology and narrative interpretation.* Albany: State University of New York Press.

Bourdieu, P. (1980). *The logic of practice.* Stanford: Stanford University Press.

Bullough, R.V. (1987). First year teaching: A case study. *Teachers College Record, 89*(2), 39-46.

Cacioppo, J.T., & Gardner, W.L. (1999). Emotion. *Annual Review of Psychology, 50,* 193-214.

Cochran-Smith, M. (2004). *Walking the road: Race, diversity and social justice in teacher education.* New York: Teachers College Press.

Cochran-Smith, M., & Zeichner, K.M. (Eds.). (2005). *Studying teacher education: The report of the AERA panel on research and teacher education.* Mahwah: Lawrence Erlbaum Associates.

Duncan-Andrade, J. (2004). Toward teacher development for the urban in urban teaching. *Teaching Education, 15*(4), 339-350.

Dyson, A. H. (2003). *The brothers and sisters learn to write: Popular literacies in childhood and school cultures.* New York: Teachers College Press.

Emig, J. (2001). Embodied learning. *English Education, 33*(4), 271-280.

Ferguson, K.E. (1984). *The feminist case against bureaucracy.* Philadelphia: Temple University Press.

Foucault, M. (1980). *Power-knowledge: Selected interviews and other writings, 1972–1977.* New York: Pantheon Books.

———. (1986). Of other spaces (J. Miskowiec, Trans.). *Diacritics, 16(1),* 22–27.

Garmon, M.A. (2004). Changing preservice teachers' attitudes/beliefs about diversity: What are the critical factors? *Journal of Teacher Education, 55*(3), 201-213.

Gerth, H. H., & Mills, C.W. (1953). *Character and social structure: The psychology of social institutions.* New York: Harcourt, Brace.

Goffman, E. (1959). *The presentation of self in everyday life.* New York: Anchor Books.

Golby, M. (1996). Teachers' emotions: An illustrated discussion. *Cambridge Journal of Education, 26*(3), 423-464.

Hargreaves, A. (2000). Mixed emotions: Teachers' perceptions of the interactions with students. *Teaching and Teacher Education, 16*(8), 811-826.

———. (2001). The emotional geographies of teaching. *Teachers' College Record, 103*(6), 1056-1080.

———. (1998). The emotional practice of teaching. *Teaching and Teacher Education, 14*(8), 835-854.

Hatfield, E., Cacioppo, J.T., & Rapson, R.L. (1994). *Emotional contagion.* New York: Cambridge University Press.

Hochschild, A. (1983). *The managed heart: The commercialization of human feeling.* Berkeley: University of California Press.

Hocking, B., Haskell, J., & Linds, W. (Eds.). (2001). *Unfolding bodymind: Exploring possibility through education.* Brandon: Foundation for Educational Renewal.

hooks, b. (1994). *Teaching to transgress: Education as the practice of freedom.* New York: Routledge.

Howard, G. (2006). *We can't teach what we don't know.* New York: Teachers College Press.

Jaggar, A. (1989). Emotion and feminist epistemology. In A. Jaggar & S. Bordo (Eds.), *Gender/body/knowledge: Feminist reconstructions of being and knowing.* New Brunswick: Rutgers University Press.

Kelchtermans, G. (1999). Teacher vulnerability. Understanding its moral and political roots. *Cambridge Journal of Education, 26*(3), 307-324.

Kemper, T.D. (1978). *A social interaction theory of emotions.* New York: John Wiley.

Ladson-Billings, G. (2005). Is the team all right? Diversity and teacher education. *Journal of Teacher Education, 56*(3), 229-234.

Ladson-Billings, G., & Tate, W. (Eds.). (2006). *Education research and the public interest: Social justice, action, and policy.* New York: Teachers College Press.

Lazarus, R.S. (1991). Cognition and motivation in emotion. *American Psychologist, 46*(4), 352-367.

———. (1999). *Stress and emotion: A new synthesis.* New York: Springer.

Leland, C.H., & Harste, J.C. (2005). Doing what we want to become: Preparing new urban teachers. *Urban Education, 40*(1), 60-77.

Lefebvre, H. (1991). *The production of space.* Oxford: Blackwell.

Lupton, D. (1998). *The emotional self: A sociocultural exploration.* London: Sage.

Mehrabian, A. (1971). *Silent messages.* Belmont: Wadsworth.

———. (1981). *Silent messages: Implicit communication of emotions and attitudes.* Belmont: Wadsworth.

Miller, s., & Norris, L. (2007). *Unpacking the loaded teacher matrix: Negotiating space and time between university and secondary English classrooms.* New York: Peter Lang.

Mottet, T., & Beebe, S. A. (2000, November). *Emotional contagion in the classroom: An examination of how teacher and student emotions are related.* Paper presented at the annual meeting of the National Communication Association Seattle.

Nias, J. (1989). *Primary teachers talking: A study of teaching and work.* London: Routledge.

———. (1993). Changing times, changing identities: Grieving for a lost self. In R.G. Burgess (Ed.), *Educational research and evaluation: For policy and practice?* (pp. 139-156). London: Farmer Press.

———. (1996). Thinking about feeling: The emotions in teaching. *Cambridge Journal of Education, 26*(3), 293-306.

Palmer, P. (1998). *The courage to teach: Exploring the inner landscape of a teacher's life.* San Francisco: Jossey-Bass.

Rogers, D.L., & Babinski, L.M. (2002). *From isolation to conversation: Supporting new teachers' development.* Albany: State University of New York Press.

Russell, J.A., & Mehrabian. (1978). Approach-avoidance and affiliation as functions of the emotion-eliciting quality of an environment. *Environment and Behavior, 10*(3), 355-387.

Schmidt, M. (2000). Role, theory, emotions, and identity in the department hardship of secondary schooling. *Teaching and Teacher Education, 16*(8), 827-842.

Soja, E.W. (1996). *Thirdspace: Journeys to Los Angeles and other real-and-imagined places.* Malden: Blackwell.

VanVeen, K., & Sleegers, P. (2006). How does it feel? Teachers' emotions in a context of change. *Journal of Curriculum Studies, 38*(1), 85-111.

Winograd, K. (2003). The functions of teacher emotions: The good, the bad, and the ugly. *Teachers College Record, 105*(9), 1641-1673.

Zembylas, M. (2003). Caring for teacher emotion: Reflections on teacher self-development. *Studies in Philosophy and Education, 22*(2), 103-125.

———. (2005). A pedagogy of unknowing: Witnessing unknowability in teaching and learning. *Studies in Philosophy and Education, 24*(2), 139-160.

2

It's in the Telling and the Sharing: Becoming Conscious of Social Justice through Communal Exploration

Laura Bolf Beliveau with Kristen Ogilvie Holzer
and Stephanie Schmidt

...narrative is present in myth, legend, fable, tale, novella, epic, history, tragedy, drama, comedy, mime, painting ... stained glass windows, cinema, comics, news items, conversation. Moreover, under this almost infinite diversity of forms, narrative is present in every age, in every place, in every society; it begins with the very history of mankind and nowhere is nor has been a people without narrative. All classes, all human groups, have their narratives.... Narrative is international, transhistorical, transcultural: it is simply there, like life itself. (Barthes, 1977, p. 79)

Culture, essentially, gives meaning. People need meaning at a fundamental level to sustain and authenticate existence within a specialized cultural milieu encoded in narrative and institutions. Meaning is made manifest through the metaphorical narratives and ordering discourses of a given culture within a given setting. By narrative, we mean everything from oral tradition of a creation myth to a morning recitation of the "Pledge of Allegiance." Those texts inform meaning and signify cultural identity. Discourse arbitrarily formalizes cultural metaphors into recognizable institutions like "theology" and "nationalism." It follows, then, that an English/language arts classroom represent culture in microcosm where narrative and discourse work to market meaning. As Ruth Vinz noted in her Foreword, "some stories stay with us" (p. xi). Like her poignant tale, our narratives acknowledge the multiple ways social justice articulate and create meaning in our lived classroom situations, real or imagined.

Oppositional dialectic has characterized western thought from Plato to Sartre. The myriad symbols of ideological dualities provide the foundations for institutions ranging from genocidal regimes to religious crusades. Michel Foucault argued that all institutions, from penitentiaries to schools, seek to demand obedience and punish disobedience (cited in Spierenburg, 2004, p. 626). Even benevolent institutions structured around exclusive binary rhetoric attempt to totalize the universe by defining it in terms of absolute values: logic and emotion; right and wrong; good and bad; natural and artificial; educated and ignorant; rich and poor; teacher and student; us and them. The tendency to impose oppositional rhetoric and repressive dichotomies in the classroom is at best unjust and at worst tyrannical. Of necessity, a pedagogy informed and inspired by a subjective conceptual framework of social justice will situate itself within the flux of contingency—the in-between spaces. Although we come together at various stages of our careers in the field of English/language arts, we speak with equal voice thus opening a dialogue and hopefully avoiding the opposition dialect and Cartesian duality that is often evident in hierarchical relations.

Students and teachers, complete with complicated histories, devise their own regulatory institutions relevant to their experience and values. The way in which teachers relate to students might serve as an example of larger societal reciprocity and social justice. Equitable, sustainable conversations about social justice might be best accommodated in an inclusive, courteous, malleable classroom designed to honor small-scale narratives. The dynamic of story recognizes autonomous existence, while providing a context for human experience and a platform for social justice: historical continuity, cultural identity, and social empathy.

The simple utterance, "Once upon a time..." (or its cultural equivalent) stirs a powerful incantation. At an existential level, the trinity of tale, teller, and told connects that experience peculiar to the human species. The narrative act touches "the realm in which aesthetics and ethics, politics and philosophy, religion and pedagogy, all fold together into some supreme vocation" (Jameson, 1994, p. 80). Thus, on a grand scale, narrative can both harm and heal and can thwart or sustain an agenda of social justice. According to Jean-François Lyotard's (1979) description of narrative knowledge in *The Postmodern Condition: A Report on Knowledge*, narrative manifestations represent both the problem and the solution with respect to ways of knowing.

According to Lyotard (1979), narrative can function as a "mode of legitimating" a collective body of knowledge that can be used to identify "one who knows from one who doesn't (the foreigner, the child)..." (p. 19). In other words, Lyotard (1979) notes the "lethal function of narrative" results in a hegemonic discourse or "canonic narrative" (p. 22) universally working as an institutionalized instrument of discrimination and exploitation. For example, a human being might justify the bondage and occupation of another human being by telling and retelling a perversion of a Judeo-Christian metanarrative promising an afterlife in which the bound and dispossessed inherit the earth.

By the same token, narrative privileges "traditional knowledge" that the metanarrative discourse would seek to sublimate. Solace and sanctuary may be found "not only in the meaning of the narratives it recounts, but also in the act of reciting them" (Lyotard, 1979, p. 22). By reiterating culturally valuable stories, generation after generation staves off the abjection and uncertainty imposed by totalizing discourses. Resistance organizes within culturally specific narratives. In either case, the species depends upon narrative. Narrative may well be the most nearly "universal," "natural," or "authentic" expression human beings can know. Story both incites and soothes the nocturnal dread that whispers, *This life is void of meaning.*

Yet narrating a life full of meaning is difficult given our multiple roles. All three of us are teacher *and* student. Laura teaches methods courses and works with preservice teachers while she finishes her doctoral degree. Kristen teaches high school seniors and takes advanced graduate courses at the same time. Stephanie tutors autistic children and serves as a graduate assistant while she completes her master's degree. Because of our varied roles, we feel the difficulty of managing postmodernity's goals. St. Pierre (2001) wisely acknowledges the limitations of defining women separately from all else indicating that it "simply doesn't work" (p. 160). Like St. Pierre (2001), we "seek out different language and practice to make sense of living" (p. 160). For us, we purposefully erase the Cartesian split between public/private, rational/emotional, and teacher/student. All aspects of our lives affect our English/language arts pedagogy, especially as it pertains to our understanding of social justice. Britzman (2003) notes, "…because teachers were once students in compulsory education, their sense of the teacher's world is strangely established before they begin learning to teach" (p. 1). She also believes that teachers' personal biographies may prohibit them from recognizing how their students' life stories may vary from their own.

Perhaps most poignantly from an adolescent perspective, "story captures our sense of ourselves and others as developing moral agents, with pasts, presents, and futures" (Kreiswirth, 2000, p. 309). From every angle, the transmission of narrative has practical implications for the English/language arts. Lyotard (1979) describes the "music" of the narrative as an exchange involving "know-how," "knowing how to speak," and "knowing how to hear" (p. 21). Plato's allegory of the cave, "recounts how and why men yearn for narratives and fail to recognize knowledge" (Lyotard, 1979, p. 29), yet the metaphorical persistence of the "tabula rasa" has historically dominated classroom teaching methodology. Neither teacher nor student possesses a blank slate, thus the importance of exchanging the respective texts of experience.

Thoroughly embedded in the dynamic of cultural exchange, conscious and unconscious narrative threads are woven through critical pedagogy. Conscious expressions and discussions of narrative, both as story and as discursive rhetoric, belong in the secondary English classroom. Harnessing the positive power of storytelling can contribute both to the holistic objectives of reading, writing, listening, and speaking and to an actualization of social justice within a secondary English classroom culture. Perhaps ironically, subjectivity lends authenticity to narrative:

> The significance of narrative is not latent in the data of experience, or of imagination, but fabricated in the process of subjecting that data to the elemental rhetoric of the narrative form itself. The categorical difference between real and imagined events is overwhelmed by the artificiality of narrative representation in either case: all narrativity, from this point of view, shares in the properties of fictionality. (Walsh, 2003, p. 111)

Encouraging students to think critically about the narratives to which they consciously and unconsciously ascribe truly begins to actualize democratic principles and make visible the metaphor of social justice. Valuing a student's story demonstrates a willingness to value the student. Through the vital medium of narrative, young adults might feel empowered by the knowledge that their experience matters within a global context. Silencing stories strips people of an essential agency. Superimposing an authoritarian narrative cripples democratic ideals.

Narrative operates as the lowest common denominator in the process of meaning-making. "Storied forms of knowledge" enable human beings to make sense of the world (Kreiswirth, 2000, p. 312). Grappling with the sheer vastness of the "discursive species" beyond ones immediate experience, human beings beg for the containment of the narrative (Lyotard, 1979). Narrative has implications far beyond the discursive confines of plot, fiction, realism, myth, fable, tale, story, history, ideology, causality, or inscrutable text. Social justice pedagogy may be actualized in narrative reciprocity, through what Lyotard (1979) calls the "little narratives" (p. 60). Instead of merely reproducing grand narratives, we encourage every classroom participant to share a story and to acknowledge all stories told within the classroom space. By doing so, we recognize the significance of sj Miller's assertion, "When we speak about social justice pedagogy, we mean that we believe all students, regardless of their differences, should be treated fairly and equitably in schools" (p. 2). Such a treatment begins with listening to *every* story.

Herein lies the framework for our chapter. Instead of remaining in our individual marked spaces (Laura as teacher educator, Kristen as novice teacher, and Stephanie as preservice teacher), we opted to make the experience communal. We strove to remove boundaries and binaries from the conversation. At the same time, we hoped to investigate the "theory/praxis nexus" (Lather, 1991, p. 27). Lather (1991) talks in terms of collective self-studies, a less oppressive, more feminist way of understanding; specifically, this methodology "models a way of doing inquiry that promotes new forms of subjectivity via a refusal of individuality and a diffusion of the sites and practices from which domination can be challenged" (p. 96). The narrative reciprocity in this chapter hopes to make the act of becoming a communal one.

Telling Our Stories

Each of us wrote a response to "What from my past articulates my understanding of social justice?" Once again, we chose to share our narratives in a collective research community. In essence, we use our reflexive ethnographies, what Ellis and Bochner (2003) call personal experiences in order to "research from one's own experience…where the researcher's experience is actually studied along with other participants…" (p. 211). Each narrative was shared and discussed by the three of us. This communal experience occurred with the context of what Ellis and Bochner (2003) call "self-discovery" or "self-creation" (p. 221).

Laura's Narrative

I am a teacher educator with experience supervising student teachers and teaching undergraduate English/language arts methodology courses. I taught high school English for sixteen years in a variety of settings—inner-city, suburban, and rural. At the time of writing this narrative, I was finishing a dissertation on beginning teachers' emotional experiences with difference. My narrative connects an event from an undergraduate literature methods course to my attempt to locate, from my personal history, events that articulate my understanding of social justice.

> Recently, I was trying so hard to make a point in an undergraduate methods course. Telling a personal teaching story, I referenced a former student who was highly effeminate and a target for much hate speak during his middle and high school years. After class, two students waited to confront me with, "Not all effeminate men are gay."
>
> On the defensive, I tried so hard to make my point, prove myself—but for what reason? Why did I protest so much, try to change their minds? Left that night feeling uneasy, feeling uncertain.
>
> Later, I reread Lucille Clifton's "here yet be dragons." Who is this "…monster whose teeth/are sharp and sparkle with lost/people, lost poems?" Am I that monster? What people have been lost to me, or, as Clifton says, "have fallen/off the edge of the world/into the dragon's mouth?" Was I a monster so busy proving my assertion that I lost the what these students wanted to say?

I must think back, imagine those times when the power of difference moved me, forced me to imagine the other. Maybe those times can inform a pedagogy that imagines the unimagined…

Popular teacher, known for her political correctness. Often asked to intervene when issues of prejudice emerge. Began the American literature class the same as all those other years: "How do we define ourselves as Americans? Do we believe in the American Dream?" Latino male student at end of class, handing me his textbook:

"*This book is wrong.*"

"*Why?*"

"*It only has stuff from the United States.*"

"*This is American literature.*"

"*American literature means literature from all the Americas.*"

"*What do you mean?*"

"*Latin America, South America.*"

He hands me the book, walks out the door and never return.

***

Sitting in a master's program, studying English as a second language/bilingual pedagogy; the only monolingual student. Often the instructor switches to Spanish, makes a joke, all the students laugh but me. Wondering if this will be on the test. Now in English, asked about my culture. Said I didn't have one. More laughter. No, really, I have no culture. Yes, yes, you do. Your culture is the only one valued in this country. What do you mean? Only the white culture matters. Me: but there is no white culture!

***

Road trip to the college town where underage drinking was no big deal. Met the coolest girl. Hung out with her all night. She asked for me to go home with her. Said we were heading home that night; maybe we'll hook up later. Friends laughing— "What? What?" She's gay, Laura. She wants to take you home. "What? What!"

***

Got punched once in high school. Black girl punched me in the arm, told me to stay away from her cousin. Loved that boy, with his dark skin and undying infatuation for me. Talked on the phone forever, until mom found out he was Black. Started going to a friend's house to use her phone. Caught mother, in hushed tones, telling my grandmother, "He's black!" Those funny nigger jokes, often told by my extended family, suddenly were pointed at me. "How's your boyfriend, Laura?"

***

But imagine this. This Catholic girl became one of the first female altar servers. Back then they had been called altar boys and I sat there, every mass, feeling that slow burn. Why were only men up there? Caused quite a stir. The very conservative Chicago diocese of the time decided we girls could carry the cross but not the host. Could carry the sign of Christ, but not his body. Long-standing church members fled the parish. But I had won, hadn't I?

In her poem, Lucille Clifton (1995) asks, "who/among us can speak with so fragile/tongue can remain proud?" Social justice is not mine alone. My pride, my attempt to change my students' minds only erases their personal history. Our collective histories matter in the classroom. If only we can imagine ourselves in the context of each other…

Kristen's Narrative

At the time of writing this narrative, I had recently finished my first year of teaching English at a large public suburban high school. My teaching assignment comprised of American Literature and Senior English. I am also a doctoral student in educational studies. This narrative tells of my educational experiences by focusing on my memorable teachers, my own rebellion against the educational machine, and my subsequent feelings as I began my own teaching career.

Both of my parents were university professors. One of my family's favorite stories tells of my ability to recite nursery rhymes (incessantly) as a toddler. Moved by rhythm and lulled by rhyme long before I could read, I rocked back and forth in the car (we called it "bouncing") chanting Mother Goose. Given a sufficient audience, my lyrical precociousness knew no bounds. Innate intelligence, lifetime education, and enduring readership were unquestionable family values.

My grandmother was wise. In our bright yellow bedroom, we talked for hours about the horrific injustice of slavery, the indiscriminate poverty of the Great Depression, and the mind-numbing hatred behind the Holocaust. In her many years, she had somehow made sense of a century that defied meaning.

As my formal education began in earnest, I would again and again be reminded of my early promise. My failure to appreciate my parent's version of my inherited potential was a betrayal, echoed in appeals punctuated by guilt. I simply refused to do anything that was asked of me — even art projects or creative ventures I ostensibly enjoyed outside of school.

Prior to the official signal to begin a standardized test in the first grade, I made the appalling decision to "connect the dots" rather than to follow the myriad directions endlessly droned from the front of the classroom. This crime was unprecedented and unforgivable. I do not remember the event, per se, but I vividly recollect the shameful aftermath. While my family was most pained by my failure to appreciate that such tests would determine my future placement levels, I saw that my teachers were most injured by my "failure to listen and follow directions."

Regardless of the circumstances, it was unacceptable for anyone in my family to appear stupid.

Perhaps most poignantly, I refused to read. It was not a matter of "can't," rather it was a matter of "won't." This rejection of the written word was incomprehensible to the entire family. Framed in fond recollections of my toddler talent for recitation and pleasing, my family expressed their anxieties about my having forgotten the former and abandoned the latter. I was baffled as to how I could have fallen so far from the tree. These seemingly deliberate deficits would come to shape my adolescent identity. I lacked some essential card dealt to the rest of my family.

But there were moments — Proustian remembrances of sneaking away from the History of Science Collections with my mother's major professor, Duane Roller. Smoke and mirrors—images of antiquity, the history of ideas, and yucky black licorice candies I was afraid to refuse. Slide after slide, through a warm curtain of swirling cigarette smoke, narrated the evolution of western thought. And I remember the questionable deeds of Lord Elgin and that even scholars mispronounced his name (Dr. Roller insisted that the "g" in question was a hard "g"). He challenged me to argue the blackness of crows. Gruffly introducing a host of characters, real and mythological, he took for grated my interest, comprehension, and engagement.

And Dr. Roller did not know about me. He did not know of my staggering failures in the classroom. I could not have been more than eight years old, but his lessons endure. Coloring my perception to this day, I will forever be captivated by the notion that my shadowy self is but a reflection cast upon a globe composed of "imperfect copies of perfect ideas." And Socrates and Plato will endure in my mind as Greek heroes, while Aristotle will never escape his role as villain.

And then there was the world of school. I was an extremely poor student primarily because I did not do anything that was asked of me. Nothing. Adolescence was particularly painful for me, but there were isolated and peculiar moments of clarity. In tenth grade I read a novel called, *The Catcher in the Rye.* I read a novel. Somewhere deep within my uncertain teenage consciousness, I found that I could identify with fictive experience and make it my own.

Perhaps more importantly I had an English teacher, Mrs. A., who took a special interest in me. During the summer of my tenth grade year, she invited me to help her to complete some home-improvement tasks. I am fairly certain that texturing walls with your English teacher would not be acceptable in today's litigious environment; perhaps it was even a bit unorthodox in 1985. Those informal discussions about *The Catcher in the Rye* linger in my memory as breathless exchanges of ideas amid the paint fumes. Alienated and disillusioned, we imagined how the plot of our respective lives might intersect with that of Holden Caulfield.

Who can say why I was unable to finish high school? Existential angst? Preternatural selfishness? Incapacitating soul sickness? Stultifying boredom? Unchecked laziness? Despite hyper self-consciousness, I was unable to pause those behaviors that were ultimately destructive of that self. At my mother's request, I jumped though one final standardized hoop and took my GED and my ACT before refusing to return to high school. On this occasion, I listened and followed directions. I "connected the dots" and scored reasonably well. Thus I began a fragmented series of transfers from one academic institution to another, leaving a trail of broken hearts in my wake.

Perhaps it was then that I began to glimpse the colossal presumption that lies just behind the public smile of instruction and the glacial pace of reform. Although I lacked the maturity to do anything but seethe, I began to entertain the idea of becoming a teacher of literature. Negative logic supported my infant theory of social justice pedagogy far better than any positive syllogism could evidence. I knew what I did not want to become.

So now I am content to live in the "becoming" moment. To my surprise, I was hired to teach English at a large public high school. I was assigned four sections of senior English and one of junior English. I have never learned more in my life than I have learned in this past year.

Remember that game, "Perfection?" The most electric moments in my classroom involved our trying to tease meaning out of collectively damning ideologies. Before we could fit all of the oddly-shaped pieces into their proper slots, the bell would buzz and the kids would pop up like so many plastic fragments.

Stephanie's Narrative

I am seeking English/language arts certification as part of a master's degree program. I plan on student teaching in the spring of 2008. My narrative discusses how social justice issues moved from the theoretical to the practical. I also discuss how my recent experiences may influence my future classroom.

The first words that come to mind when I hear "social justice" are "women's rights" and "gender equality." This is appropriate for someone who spent much of her undergraduate years at a small liberal arts college debating with others, mainly men, about such catch phrases as "the glass ceiling" or equality for all, regardless of gender and sexual orientation. These debates were always based on some piece of theory that was being read in an English class. They were arguments of just that: theory. I don't want to diminish my passion for these issues, but they were, after all, the ravings of a self-professed feminist who had yet to even step foot into a real classroom in the "real world."

In the last 6 months, I have come into contact with a more tangible, less theoretical situation that I see as much more applicable in my own future classroom. I have had the privilege of working with two different children with autism. Both children are male; one is four and the other is six. I have had the opportunity of shadowing the four year old, who I will call Austin, through his preschool two days a week for the last few months. My job is to help Austin as he transitions throughout the day from classroom to classroom. I am also there to help redirect him if he begins to get fixated on something he should not be playing with or if he gets frustrated. Through my own observations, and through conversations I've had with his mother, I have come to understand a more subtle type of "inequality" that I myself have most likely contributed to in the past.

Austin is a very smart four-year-old. He learns quickly, is happy to please others and could be described as functioning highly for a child with autism. And yet, when Austin's teachers hear that he has autism, they typically react in one of two ways: with fear, or with hopelessness.

During the school year, Austin's teachers did their best to understand how to help him throughout the day. But when they were faced with having Austin in their classroom alone without additional support from me or Austin's therapist, they were fearful. The word autism had already prejudiced their minds as such a negative thing, these teachers were literally afraid to be left alone with him. It was through the constant reassurance of both Austin's mom and his therapist that they were finally confident enough in their understanding of Austin. This reaction, I believe, came from a genuine desire to help Austin have the best preschool experience possible. His teachers were fearful of Austin because they did not understand him, yet they were also fearful that they would fail him.

In the last two weeks I have seen a different kind of prejudice. One of his summer school teachers did not understand Austin's autism. Austin is a very smart four year old. He has learned that there are people who will not challenge him to participate in things he does not care for if he throws a temper tantrum. This was the case in Austin's classroom this summer. Because his teacher did not understand Austin, she found it easier to spend the first few days of her class sitting in a corner by himself looking at books. Because of the word "autism," Austin was left behind by his teacher.

I talked to Austin's mother about this classroom situation and she admitted that this is a common theme among many people who meet Austin. They hear the word autism and automatically expect less of Austin's abilities. Another child, without autism, would have been expected to participate in all classroom activities. Yet, when we don't understand the differences of our students, it is easy to get distracted by the fact that some children are different.

I have learned more from these last six months of working with Austin about what social justice truly means to me as a future educator than I did in four years of undergraduate college. Social justice is not just a catch phrase for me anymore. It still incites passionate discussions on my part, but they are no longer theoretical in nature. Instead, I see social justice as referring to an active participation on my part. I have actual life experience that I now draw on when I think of my future classroom. As the rate of autism in our country continues to grow, I know that I will have one or more children with autism in my future classroom. Because of my experience with Austin, I know that I am better prepared to teach in a way that is more beneficial to a child with autism. I am sure that I would have reacted just like Austin's teachers, with fear or hopelessness, but I am excited that I now have the tools to help children like Austin to the best of my ability.

Discussion of Narratives

As stated above, we were interested in the communal aspect of sharing our stories. Could we avoid the totalizing discourses discussed by Lyotard (1979)? Likewise, would we discuss our collective self-studies in way that extends beyond traditional boundaries (Lather, 1991)? We found that our narrative reciprocity created an open space. Our discussion began solely in reference to the shared narratives, but during the sharing process, we began to ask important questions of ourselves and of our past, present, and future classrooms. Below we offer excerpts as a way to both model the communal process and consider the serious implications of social justice in the English/language arts classroom.

Excerpt 1

This part of the discussion focuses on Stephanie's narrative about her work helping children with autism. Yet it may be compelling to notice how well Kristen's experiences as both a mother and a beginning teacher relate to Stephanie's situation. Our students' perceptions of us as teachers, caretakers, individuals, and fellow learners may be vital to situating social justice within a classroom.

Laura:
  Why this narrative?

Stephanie:
  This is real to me right now. Like I say in my narrative, I have moved away from theory into what is practical in the classroom. I have this hands-on practical experience with children with autism two days a week for twelve hours a day.

Kristen:
  So you see injustice in relation to him?

Stephanie:

Talking to Austin's mom was telling. Her reaction to Austin's teacher letting him sit in the corner for two days was also telling. She said that if another child without the label "autism" had acted in the same way, they would have still been expected to participate in the classroom activity. But his diagnosis makes people uncomfortable and therefore they have a tendency to ignore him. She said, "He's not going to go away. You can't just ignore him until he disappears."

Laura:

You plan on being an English/language arts teacher, and you will have students labeled autistic, but what other students might benefit from this new understanding or the practical aspect? How would it translate for all kids in the classroom?

Stephanie:

Students are somewhat influenced by a teacher's attitude toward other children in the classroom. Even these four-year-old children in Austin's class see how the teacher reacts to Austin and then they react to him similarly. They just soak it up. It's important as a teacher to keep that in mind and act accordingly. Of course you can never do everything.

Kristen:

My daughter talks about an autistic boy she's been in school with since grade school. She judges a teacher's character or style or kindness by how they react to this kid.

Laura:

Kristen, do you think your students tested you in this same way?

Kristen:

I do. As far as patience—I think they see just how far they can push you and walk all over you. Perhaps they are interested in kindness and power, too.

Laura:

That's so true. Kids do test everything, not just how "easy" you may be or how lenient. Stephanie, do you think Austin tests people?

Stephanie:

Very much so. His throwing a temper tantrum in class was a learned behavior. He tested his teacher and learned that he didn't have to participate in activities he didn't like. He still tests me, too, even though we've worked together for five months.

Laura:

In my narrative, I felt tested by these two women who approached me and purposefully put me on the defensive. It would be easy not show kindness, you know. I don't know if you felt that way. Do you sit there and think, "I don't know how to react." How much do I reveal of myself? How much should I act in the way we are "supposed" to act?

This sense of "testing" teachers is evident in all of our situations. Stephanie noticed that Austin was testing his teachers, but Kristen wisely reminds us that students test their own limits and the teacher's limits simultaneously. This in turn helps Laura think about the students from her narrative. Were they testing Laura's commitment to social justice issues? Or, were they testing her ideology?

Austin's mother so poignantly said, "He's not going to go away. You can't just ignore him until he disappears." Perhaps this statement serves as a mantra for all students with whom we work. Our dedication to (or lack thereof) social justice issues affects all participants in the educational space. Whether we state our commitment publicly or not, our stance will most likely emerge.

Excerpt 2

As our discussion continued, we began to consider the ways in which our personal narratives, once shared, began to define us as individuals. Yet we are also willing to interrogate any fixed positioning. Stephanie asks a vital question of teaching—can we be ourselves as teachers? Kristen's educational experiences, both positive and negative, clearly influenced her pedagogy during her first year. Likewise, Laura's narrative and subsequent comments help her to better understand how her own history influenced the ways she reacted to the incident mentioned at the beginning of her piece.

Stephanie:
    Can you be like the person you are, or do have to give that up when you are teaching?

Kristen:
    That was the biggest thing I managed to learn this first year. As soon as I stopped acting like I thought I was expected to act—literally acting like in a theatrical production for me, and I'm scared of stage fright constantly—once I started being who I am, things were better. They can see that too. Perhaps, I don't know, it seems like we search so hard for the right language. How else could you portray that situation in your narrative [directed to Laura] but use the word effeminate? How else could you have said that? If we cannot have a dialogue about this stuff any more, then we can't have a dialogue at all any more. That's a problem for social justice.

Laura:
    So we try to "fix" terms. Even autism. But it's not fixed—they call it a spectrum right? On a personal level, my narrative tries to show a spectrum, where I came from. Could that articulate my work with preservice teachers? But I don't have the answers, and I feel like I must have all the answers in the college classroom. I feel like I'm acting from some kind of script. Maybe that's such a danger for teachers of all levels. Kristen, you write about not being a good student. How has your history affected your pedagogy the first year?

Kristen:

As far as kind of being all over the place, I'm not going to impose meaning which is extremely frustrated for all of us. Sometimes we'll be reading something and I just want to say, "Okay, this is it, this is what it means." But I just won't do it. I just have to bite my tongue and not do it, but it is frustrating for all of us because we don't want ambiguity. I think that has everything to do with social justice and the fact that I don't know, I can't say for sure because I was too little, but I think that I had just this, you know, abnormal dislike of authority.

I think we all try rebellion, but it just doesn't go away for me. I just don't want to be that person. In the halls I wonder why are they looking at me like this? Why does everyone hate me? Why do I feel so alienated? Just like I did in high school. It's because I'm the "man." I have this label of authority. It took me forever to get over that. It took a reputation, too: "She's cool." People were always hiding from me.

Laura:

Stephanie, are you ready to be the "man"?

Stephanie:

No. I think for the same reasons. I can't say that I was ever anti-authority, but there is a part of me that likes to argue whatever it is I believe in. I feel like that will be stifled in a way.

Laura:

Stifled by whom?

Stephanie:

Stifled by myself because I can't exactly say what it is I want to say. If it comes to the issues we are talking about here, especially in different geographical areas. You can't always say what you want to say reading a certain book or a certain short story.

Whether initiated internally or externally, censorship remains part of the teaching space. Stephanie's use of the word "stifle" is telling. Although she discusses self-censoring, it is possible that some of the grand narratives of modernity have become so ingrained that we don't completely acknowledge the institutional demands of teaching in public schools. What role does authority play in initiating social justice pedagogy? And, as the next section shows, how does this directly relate to what and how we teach?

Excerpt 3

The English/language arts classroom is full of opportunity to teach issues, literature, and writing relevant to social justice. As we found out through our discussion, our teaching positions may be stifled by personal or public censure. When presented with texts like Fredrick Douglass's slave narrative, what role should a teacher take to initiate a classroom space open to discussion? And, what problems may emerge during this process?

Laura:

People sometimes equate social justice with political correctness. I really don't want to be that person where my students have to pretend that they never had a prejudicial thought, ever. I want to be the person where they disclose that they don't know what to do. How do you do that in a classroom? How do you make it open enough?

Kristen:

I think it comes back to that. If we cannot use the language required, like power, difference, etc., and if we can't use that language, even some slurs, then we can't have a dialogue or a conversation. We can't see the power of that language. When I read Fredrick Douglass's narrative, I didn't ask them to read it. It was really, really hard and we didn't shy away. I used the "n-word" twice. It was just like something exploded in the room, several times. I thought, "I can't do this."

Laura:

Can't do what?

Kristen:

I can't say it again. I'm not going to do it. In a way, it shrank, because Douglass uses it in quotes. He equates profanity with the lashes, the raping, the other horrendous events that happen in the book. Murder among them. I just thought, I can't do this any more. Then I thought does it rob the narrative? Does it rob it? Does it take power from the message which is that language matters.

Laura:

You, me, every white woman: I think of our privileged backgrounds. Kristen, what right do you have to say that word, talk about Fredrick Douglass? Stephanie, what right do you have to talk about autism? These are questions the so-called "other" asks. For example, one of the women who confronted me is gay. Sometimes it is hard for me as a white, heterosexual married woman with the two kids and the whole happy perfect family. Do I have that right?

Stephanie:

Because of political correctness or because self-censorship, you are very limited. For example, not being able to say words in context, in a book that makes the story so powerful and adds to the narrative. Laura, I remember being in your class when you were talking about the boy from your classroom, and your point was the opposite of whatever these girls were accusing you of. I think most people in the class understood that was your point, too. But what they did and maybe what you felt was that it's not politically correct to say those things. It becomes very hard to even discuss these issues.

Laura:

I wonder if you could approach Fredrick Douglass from that angle when you were reading it in class.

Kristen:

We kind of did. We talked about the language, the power of language, the power it has to hurt you. Then when we have a narrative and I try to avoid the universal theme.

I tell them we don't play in the universal. I try to put it in a postmodernist light. I know what you are saying about your political agenda coming through. There is a point when sharing part of myself has been vital—getting to know these kids. Even what appears on the surface: married, two kids, suburbia. It sure doesn't look like I hitchhiked across the country with a backpack.

Laura:

Do you have to put yourself out there?

Kristen:

I think, to an extent. To a safe extent. Safe for them, too. I was quoted in the school newspaper. I was asked what I thought about school violence. I said, "I just can't operate in a fear-driven way. I just can't psychologically do that." Then I looked at all the politic answers of everyone else, "You have to wear IDs to make sure there aren't any outsiders in here." I was thinking, "You had to wear IDs in Nazi Germany." Then I have to say, "shut up" to myself.

Laura:

Stephanie, you talked about the words that come to mind when I hear social justice are "women's rights" and "gender equality." Are you prepared to let your stance on those come out in the classroom?

Stephanie:

Again, I think it depends a lot on where I am geographically. I feel like from where I came, I felt it was a little bit more acceptable to talk about that. We had teachers who would talk about sexual orientation and women's rights. But I don't see that as much if I stay here.

Regardless of our teaching levels, all three of us questioned how our personal beliefs should or would be discussed in the classroom. Kristen's use of the "n-word" caused her much angst. She was conscious of the students in her class and their multi-layered responses to that word. Stephanie discusses the conservative demographic in which we live. But Kristen's adamant belief that language must be confronted is telling. In our act of becoming, language marks a variety of spaces. As the next section contends, building a community first may be the first step to creating a safe space for social justice issues to emerge.

Social Justice in the Classroom

What do our personal narratives and collective discussion mean in terms of the real life application into an English/language arts classroom? Can our hope for an environment that negates hegemony and patriarchy come to fruition? If so, what would such a classroom look like?

Kristen's work with Fredrick Douglass's narrative sparked much interest in our discussion, and with her permission, we now focus on an assignment she felt reflected strong social justice pedagogy. Yet we consider this assignment as a state of becoming. Just as our narratives and the subsequent conversation informed our individual and collective meanings of social justice, this classroom assignment allows us to see social justice in practice.

This assignment began with a phone conversation between Kristen and Laura. Knowing that Laura had experience with teaching slave narratives, Kristen called asking if Laura would like to be a guest in her American Literature course. After discussing what was happening in the class, Kristen indicated that she wanted to prepare the students to understand the historical precedent of the slave narratives. Although Laura mentioned a friend's use of a quilting experience while teaching *Their Eyes Were Watching God*, Kristen took this passing comment to heart and created an assignment called "The Narrative Quilt Assignment" (see Appendix A).

The essence of the assignment focuses on vital issues related to narrative, power, and cultural identity. Students are asked to choose six scraps of material provided by Kristen and then arrange them in a way that represented different stages of their lives, were emblematic of their cultural identity and/or heritage, were symbolic of their family history, created a message or statement for the world, presented a map to freedom, or blended any combination of those suggested.

After students completed their individual quilts, each part was blended into a whole; the entire class was ultimately represented by one large quilt. The implications of the quilt were many. Kristen's own personal teaching journal recorded her impressions as the quilting assignment was implemented in the class:

> The day was a success. I was thrilled with the student's response to the Narrative Identity Quilt. They were patient and engaged and funny. They shared the scissors. They helped each other to thread their needles. They gave each other advice like, "Even though it SEEMS easier to use a long thread, you're just gonna tangle it up and have to start all over again." I couldn't help but call attention to the metaphorical relevance to the living choices we make. We will have a wonderful display of our truly diverse classroom. I hope we will move beyond "tolerance" in this lesson. I hope we will leap over "acceptance." I hope we will land smack in the middle of "appreciation" of our different experiences. Hooray, juniors! Way to piece together your American experience.
>
> ***
>
> The juniors continued with their quilting. It was a nice, busy hour. My friend is planning to come speak to my class on Friday. She is quite interested in working on a social justice curriculum. The primary focus of her research and scholarship is on issues of race and the classroom. We look forward to hearing from her.
>
> ***
>
> The juniors finished their quilting projects today. The writing came much more easily than in the past (although, I can't complain—they seem to enjoy informal, reflective writing and persuasive writing over controversial subjects). Tomorrow, we will develop definitions (as a class) related to power and difference. We will then tell our stories and show off our quilts.

***

On Friday, my friend will be our guest teacher. She's going to divide us into groups and have us look for examples of some of our classroom definitions (social justice, oppression, etc.) in Pat Mora's "Sonrisas." She also has clips of Depression era Library of Congress recordings of enslaved men and women. Narrative has come alive this week.

Kristen had positive feedback from the students. One anonymous comments was:

This quilt represents me in some odd and weird way. But never the less it is still part of me. This quilt has been made by my own hands, my own sweat and blood. I will always remember the time I made a quilt in English.

In response to student reactions, Kristen writes:

I am most amazed by this kind of acceptance that has graced this week. Some things have worked, some things have not. That's just alright, today. Do you ever wish you could just "teach" surrender and acceptance? It's just a more reasonable way to live. Nope—I have to fight and struggle and finally submit to life on lifes terms. I just feel like I've had a breakthrough! I can have a less that wonderful day in the classroom and not be consumed by remorse. I don't want to compromise my standards, but what good am I if I am morbidly reflecting about a day I cannot rewind?

A different sense of narrative reciprocity operates here. First, Kristen's assignment allows students a narrative of their own. Not unlike the narratives Laura, Kristen, and Stephanie created for this chapter, Kristen's students were allowed a sense of personal history, both personal and public, that eventually created a place from which to address Fredrick Douglass's narrative. By allowing her students to create a personal understanding of who they are, even in the metaphoric sense, Kristen's subsequent reading of the narrative was one of the most powerful experiences of the class. As one of her journal entries notes, "We decided that Frederick Douglass was simply one of the greatest minds our nation has produced."

Whereas this assignment may seem particular to high school American literature, we see applications in myriad settings. Laura's narrative referenced an event from an undergraduate methods course. The disconnect between her intended message and the one perceived by two of her students may show the need to create a safe place from which to discuss issues of social justice and difference. Instead of a narrative quilt, these preservice teachers could write narratives that traced their own experience with difference. This "telling" of their stories could result in a sharing that creates a community where dissonance is discussed openly and understanding reached through the theory/practice nexus (Lather, 1991).

Stephanie's narrative may illuminate this process. Her work with Austin, a boy with autism, pushes her to truly engage in an emancipatory praxis (see

Lather, 1991). Her narrative first establishes her stance. As Lather (1991) contends, "To position my own discourse is to mark a place from which to speak" (p. 8). From this place, she then takes her undergraduate educational underpinnings and interrogates them in terms of her experiences with Austin. Eventually she arrives here, "…I see social justice as referring to an active participation on my part…I have actual life experience that I now draw on when I think of my future classroom." Just as Kristen's students could draw on their quilting experiences while she read the Douglass narrative, Stephanie uses her narrative as basis for understanding social justice in the classroom.

Some Final Thoughts

The processes we undertook for this chapter have helped to articulate our ways of telling, sharing, and embodying social justice. We found that the communal experience helped each of us to understand social justice in a broader sense. In essence, by telling and sharing our narratives, we located a site where we felt empowered to engage in the five "re-s" outlined in sj Miller's Introduction: reflect, reconsider, reconceptualize, rejuvenate, and to reengage (p. 7). Hence we reached a space where we could consider our varied teaching praxes.

Although we entered into this experience knowing one another, we still felt some apprehension putting ourselves in a public space. Obviously, that fear still exists as we consider our future classrooms. Each of us, however, is committed to the act of becoming, and we each leave this experience having advanced our "becoming" in the variety of roles we live each day: mother, daughter, friend, teacher, colleague, student, academic, wife, partner, and learner. Yet we conclude here with some final comments from our respective "places."

Laura

The incident that begins my narrative marked a turning point in my understanding of how social justice issues matter in the public classroom space. My immediate response was defensive in nature, yet this erased my own history. Instead of drawing from my experiences, they went unrealized. Simultaneously, I erased my students' histories. Instead of engaging in a conversation about language, power, and social justice, our voices were silenced.

As Kristen, Stephanie and I talked, we marked certain places where our own best intentions fail from our own fear. Whether we silence ourselves purposefully or not, our narrated pasts articulate our pedagogy. Opening spaces in careful and collective ways may allow a dialogue not yet heard. Unable to go back in time to redress that moment, I only can consider ways this communal experience may change my future pedagogical decisions. Whereas I still do not want to be the "politically correct" teacher, I now recognize my own quest for social justice in my own life. My students' quests will not mirror mine. But their voices, as Lucille Clifton (1995) poem states, must never fall into the dragon's mouth.

Kristen

When my students ask me why I am "making them read this stuff" or why I "make them write every day," my response is reflexive in the reactionary sense of the word: "If you don't learn how to read and write your world, someone else will read it and write it for you!" Reading and writing then becomes a bit subversive and revolutionary. We do not accept imposed meaning in my classroom and we do not shrink from the good fight. We are dangerous.

Among the myriad "strategies" and top-down paradigms for motivating student engagement and achievement, I have never heard, "Teach and learn to critically question and problematize what you read and hear through what you write and say." Social justice pedagogy teaches both teachers and students to read, write, and speak the text of a world to which they are profoundly connected.

Thus, reflexivity in the sense of deeply understanding the narrative of self that one brings to the classroom, the story of the self as researcher, is much more than being honest about the values and biases of that self. Narrative reflexivity for practitioners of social justice pedagogy is yet another fiction, but it is a self conscious fiction. We cannot escape the fictionality of the text, but we can foster the dynamic exchange of stories that give voice to the broad spectrum of experience outside of the containment and imposition of the grand narrative.

Listening, telling, writing, and reading the narratives of social justice pedagogy with my colleagues for this chapter did not result in any decisive, teleological revelation about myself as a practitioner. Rather, our shared experience gave rise to the kind of inquiry social justice pedagogy seeks to further. As is inevitably the case in my classroom, I learned infinitely more than I taught in the telling of my experience of social justice pedagogy.

Stephanie

I've always been aware of my social justice in my personal life, but I don't know if I've ever been forced to stop and think about how that will effect my pedagogy in the future. We discuss issues in classes, but they often have a theoretical bent to them. Questions like "what if" or "how will I handle this" are the norm in teacher education classes, especially undergraduate ones, because we have very little real life experience to base these conversations on.

The class that challenged me the most to take stock of my social justice pedagogy was a young adult literature class. Being able to read different characters' life experiences, even if they were fictional, sparked heated debates and respectful conversations. I only wonder if all pre-service teachers have the opportunity to really stop and take stock of their own thoughts on social justice pedagogy.

In my sharing with the Laura and Kristin, I was able to put these thoughts that began forming last fall into concrete words and ideas. I think it was through hearing these women's experiences that I was then able to let my own values grow. The classes that I've taken with practicing teachers have also allowed me to stretch my own beliefs as I learn through their stories.

At Last

Patti Lather (1991) says of her own text,

> I have, however, attended to what Derrida…speaks of as "writing under erasure." What this means to me is that to write "postmodern" is to write paradoxically aware of one's own complicity in that which one critiques. Such a movement of reflexivity and historicity at once inscribes and subverts…". (p. 10)

It is our hope that we continually engage in a communal act of becoming and understanding ourselves. Lucille Clifton so eloquently states, "who/among us can imagine ourselves/unimagined?" We wish to honor both our students' and our own stories, never to be erased, always to be imagined as valuable elements of the educational space.

References

Barthes, R. (1977). *Image—music—text*. New York: Hill & Wang.

Britzman, D.P. (2003). *Practice makes practice: A critical study of learning to teach* (revised ed.). Albany: State University of New York Press.

Clifton, L. (1995). Here yet be dragons. In C. Merrill & C. Buckley (Eds.), *What will suffice: Contemporary American poets on the art of poetry* (p. 18). Layton: Gibbs Smith Publishers.

Ellis, C., & Bochner, A.P. (2003). Autoethnography, personal narrative, reflexivity: Researcher as subject. In N.K. Denzin & Y.S. Lincoln (Eds.), *Collecting and interpreting qualitative material* (2nd Ed.) (pp. 199-258). Thousand Oaks: Sage.

Jameson, F. (1994). *The seeds of time*. New York: Columbia University Press.

Kreiswirth, M. (2000). "Merely telling stories? Narrative and knowledge in the human sciences." *Poetics Today, 21*(2) 293-318.

Lather, P. (1991). *Getting smart: Feminist research and pedagogy with/in the postmodern*. New York: Routledge.

Lyotard, J. (1979). *The postmodern condition: A report on knowledge*. Minneapolis: University of Minnesota Press.

Spierenburg, P.C. (2004). "Punishment, power, and history: Foucault and Elias." *Social Science History, 28*(4) 607-636.

St. Pierre, E.A. (2001). Coming to theory: Finding Foucault and Deleuze. In K. Weiler (Ed.), *Feminist engagements: Reading, resisting, and revisioning male theorists in education* (pp. 141-163). New York: Routledge.

Walsh, R. (2003). "Fictionality and mimesis: Between narrativity and fictional worlds." *Narrative, 11*(1) 111-121.

Appendix A

Narrative Identity Quilt

Please take this project seriously. I want you to have fun and express yourselves, but know that I am interested in your visualization of some very vital issues related to narrative, power, and cultural identity. Don't waste class time, friends. As always, I will be delighted to help you during any phase of this project. "But Ms. Holzer, I'm a dude," will not excuse you from participating. A quilt is a METAPHOR. **This project is worth a total of 200 points.**

Part I: Quilt Square

1. Choose AT LEAST six (6) fabric scraps that you consider representative of:
   a. stages of your life OR
   b. emblematic of your cultural identity/heritage OR
   c. symbolic of your familial history OR
   d. a message/statement you would like to send the world OR
   e. a map to freedom OR
   f. any combination of the above

2. Position the scraps so that they become descriptive or symbolic of the message you are trying to relate.

3. Tack the pieces together with large loose stitches (your classmates and I will help you).

4. Use smaller, finer stitches to complete your square (your classmates and I will help you).

Part II: Written Narrative
In AT LEAST one full page, explain the significance of the choices you've made for you square. You need a creative and relevant TITLE for your square.

Part III: Presented Narrative
Fifty points of extra credit will be available to all students who choose to present their squares to the class and explain their significance.

Scoring Rubric:

HAND IN THIS PROJECT DESCRIPTION AND RUBRIC WITH YOUR PROJECT.
Be sure your name is on this sheet.

_____ 180-200: The artist has provided detailed images and language to depict events, represent characters, and/or express themes. Time and care has been taken to produce a quality piece of creative expression.

_____ 160-180: The artist has provided some detailed images and language depict events, represent characters, and/or express themes. Some time and care has been taken to produce a quality piece of creative expression.

_____ 140-160: The artist has provided minimally detailed images and language depict events, represent characters, and/or express themes. Minimal time and care has been taken to produce a quality piece of creative expression.

_____ 120-140: The artist has not seriously considered this project. She or he has likely produced the piece in the car on the drive to school.

3

Quiet Tensions in Meaning:
A Conversation with a "Social Justice"
Teacher

David Kirkland with Danielle Filipiak

A permissive beauty is struck in science through story. Never more clearly is this beauty captured than when we hear with inquisitive ears the etchings of the human soul and its strivings crafted carefully in a symphony of many voices made known through singular testimonies. Such testimonies can be "a profound form of scholarship moving serious study close to the frontiers of art" (Featherstone, 1989, p. 377). As we hope to illustrate in this chapter primarily using Danielle's testimony as an example, it is only possible to understand the meanings of complex concepts like teaching and justice through our stories. As we both discovered, it isn't quite as easy to negotiate what it means to teach for justice in our pedagogical present where notions of justice are either constantly under siege or continually under debate (North, 2006).

Danielle's story helps us, if only to piece together parts of the debate, to draw out an element of the internal and external tension housed in the meaning of justice. At moments in her story, Danielle recalls encounters with an abundance of pedagogical ideas put forth in the name of social justice, primarily to reconcile pain and social injury. These ideas did not always mean the same things. Together, Danielle and I seek to understand how these ideas gained meaning, especially at points of incongruence, where Danielle's transition between preservice and inservice teaching spaces highlighted such tensions. Her role in this narrative is as storyteller. My story is also told, but only in relation to Danielle's story and our struggle to make sense of social justice teaching.

We frame our chapter as a dialogue, for in communication we locate meanings and the complexities that lie therein. According to North (2006), "When communication is understood as a historical complex chain of calls and responses, the notion of the purely autonomous individual falls away, as the individual is always responding to an/other, whether in the form of other individual or groups of human beings or historical, institutionalized, authoritative, and/or internally persuasive discourses" (p. 526). In this conversation, we seek to respond to two questions: How have negotiating competing ideas of social justice contributed to Danielle's transition from preservice to inservice teaching? And how are the tensions present in competing meanings of "social justice" resolved in Danielle's story?

As she struggled to define social justice in her teaching and as those struggles were made manifest through our conversation, we hope to illustrate for readers the complex ways in which Danielle placed the ideas, the many voices that framed her understanding of social justice into dialogue with what she felt was just to her students. This dialogic, or constant struggle between *internally persuasive discourse* and *authoritative discourse* (Bakhtin, 1981), created a tension within Danielle with which she never easily comes to terms. On the one hand there is her personal story—how she experienced school. On the other hand there is her story with others—how the things around Danielle helped her to make sense of school. As she experienced school in many locations, Danielle could neither locate justice within or outside herself. For her, the meaning of justice emerged contingent and yet remained tenuous in the intersections of passion and pain.

The tension in meaning found in Danielle's story, we suggest calls for constant conversation—internal and external dialogue—about the meanings of justice and a willingness to revise these meanings to accommodate the practical demands of actual situations, the honest feeling of real people, and the realities of our common circumstances. Further, we maintain that the voyage from preservice to inservice teaching spaces is one complicated by these tensions, in part, due to the uncertainty masked in meanings, collisions of interests attached to words, and the ever-shifting tilt in our understandings of why we social justice teachers teach.

Finally, we are tempted by regret because the story that is told is not about social justice teaching, *per se.* We offer no radical lesson plans to transform our societies. We provide no solutions to the problems plaguing our profession, our classrooms, or our world. Instead, we simply offer a story about meaning. This story about meaning highlights a conversation about justice, a conversation that began with a single question.

Why Did You Get into Teaching? Beginning a Conversation about Meaning and Justice

"Why did you get into teaching?" Danielle asked me.

I answered with poetic passion and uncertain certainty, "I teach for justice out of the bowels of struggle to make sure all children are guaranteed a better education than I received."

I grew up in Detroit, MI, a product of a fractured educational system, still reeling from years of neglect, the scars of racial and social injustice, and the plight of the postindustrial moment. Detroit, like most large urban school districts, was met with fierce dilemmas throughout the eighties and early nineties due to radical alterations in the American economy, racial and social demographic shifts due to White and middle-class Black flight from the central city, and chronically poor municipal management. In addition, a large number of Detroit's teachers commuted to the city for work and departed from the city after work. Hence, there was little connection between my schools, my community, and me.

Having successfully navigated a large urban school district, which I must admit taught me much, I enrolled in college wanting to teach. Not just teach, however. I wanted to teach for justice, which to me meant helping to create educational conditions—curricular and pedagogical—that reconnected schools, communities, and individuals to larger civic and economic aspirations. Teaching, I thought, was about more than dictating privileged ideas or overseeing the social sorting process. Rather, for me, it was a powerful profession, essential for promoting new ideas or proliferating existing ones. Since teaching seemed so powerful yet political, becoming a teacher was about changing my world or at least the world of others who existed in conditions similar to the ones in which I was raised.

Although I well understood the reasons why I got into teaching, my response to Danielle weaved around a question not easily answered. Though it proved a sturdy response reflective of my good intentions, my answer was vague. It lacked clear meaning, troubled by the inherent ambiguities found in words, especially in word like justice. So I pondered, "What is justice? And how does one teach for it?"

While it does not answer these questions, the reason that I provided for going into teaching, one might suggest, was not tied to changing my students' presents, but to amending my own pasts. Justice, for me, was a concept that appropriated an idea populated in my story, my interests, and my meanings of the world. Hence, it meant working to replace my educational experiences with something "better." As Ruth Vinz so eloquently points out in her foreword to this text, teachers teach in response to the living histories hidden and unhidden within them. Hence, I was not being fraudulent in my response nor was I being pretentious by it. Justice found meaning for me within. From within, justice, to me, implied struggle, and struggle implied a guarantee for "a better education," a changed world. The question remained, however, for whom?

The conversation continued with me elaborating on my initial response:

David: Justice is the condition of fairness, where educating all youth is a fundamental right and responsibility for all, especially in a democracy.

> **Danielle:** I believe in everything that you're saying, but every teacher I know says the same thing that she or he "teaches for justice." But how do you teach for justice? Do you transform standards, or do you make sure students meet existing standards? It seems like we can all agree that justice might mean a fair education for everyone. I even heard George W. Bush say that *No Child Left Behind* was supposed to guarantee a fair education for all students, but in my classes at Michigan State University, we critiqued NCLB for promoting inequity. So what's fair? I guess I need to know not only what justice looks like as a product, educated youth, but what justice look like as a process, educating youth. When I first went into the classroom, I thought I was teaching for justice when I had my students do a lot of interesting things like read raps as poetry. But my students had to take tests—too many of them. Many of my students, in spite of how well I thought they were doing in my classes, failed the tests. Here I am thinking social justice teaching means transforming students' lives by transforming my English classroom, but I had to come to terms with the fact that my student were being held accountable for a curriculum and a classroom that was not being transformed. So my changing the curriculum was not fair to them. I could have continued to buck the system, being that rogue, revolutionary teacher that Michigan State University prepared me to be, but—at the end of the day—my students were subject to that system. Ultimately, I would have been hurting them. Given my responsibilities to students, I am not really sure what social justice teaching means.

Like me, Danielle was struggling to make sense of justice through her story. She used her personal classroom experiences, both preservice and inservice, to interpret what I meant by "justice." She appropriated the term from me and from others and from her experiences teaching, agreeing that justice as a product, as some recognizable end, meant a "fair education" for all youth. However, Danielle was unsure as to what justice meant as a process, as a means of fairly educating particular youth like her students. So unlike me, Danielle did not enjoy the luxury of an impassioned and idealized notion of justice divorced from the complexities of her actual teaching situation. As a result, she ran into problems defining it.

We knew from our conversation that defining justice was complex (Ayers, Hunt, & Quinn, 1998; Cochran-Smith, Davis, & Fries, 2003; Pang & Gibson, 2001), indeed, made complicated by the dynamism of language. We understood in a fine Bakhtinian (1981, 1986) way that words are relative, based on an ongoing dialogue between texts and their contexts. Within this dialogue, a tension in meaning arises. However, the delicate vagueness in a word is welcomed as a way of creating meanings that are socially derived through the shared medium of conversation where ideas are exchanged (Bakhtin, 1986; Greenleaf & Katz, 2004).

For Bakhtin (1981, 1986), a term or idea takes on a life beyond itself as it is uttered. The meaning of an *utterance*, a thought given voice, is embodied within a speaker and integrated within a *discourse*, a feature of language that delineates a form of social life. It is in this way that every utterance is also internally dialogic, for in Bakhtin's (1986) view, all speech is linked to the words, ideas, and utterances of others. According to Bakhtin (1981),

Discourse lives, as it were, beyond itself, in a living impulse [*napravlennost'*] toward the object; if we detach ourselves completely from this impulse all we have left is the naked corpse of the word, from which we can learn nothing at all about the social situation or the fate of a given word in life. *To study the word as such, ignoring the impulse that reaches out beyond it, is just as senseless as to study psychological experience outside the context of that real life toward which it was directed and by which it is determined.* (p. 292, emphasis in the original)

Every discourse, then, is twice dialogized. While it carries within itself the utterances and ideas of others, it gains life within a specific situation when addressed to a specific audience. However, no utterance, and by extension no idea, arrives at definition within the immediate audience alone. A degree of meaning is retained in the word, and relates to a guiding presence that a speaker addresses beyond the immediate context and audience. According to Bakhtin (1986),

[T]he author of the utterance, with a greater or lesser awareness, presupposes a higher superaddressee (third), whose absolutely just responsive understanding is presumed, either in some metaphysical distance or in distant historical time (the loophole addressee). In various ages and with various understandings of the world, this superaddressee and his ideally true responsive understanding assume various ideological expresstion . . . . (p. 126)

How we choose to refer to this presence—whether it be "God, absolute truth, the court of dispassionate human conscience, the people, the court of history, [or] science" (Bakhtin, 1986, p. 126)—does not matter.

What does matter is the Bakhtinian belief that all discourse was impossible without the existence of such a presence. This presence, Bakhtin (1986) argues, need not be "mystical or metaphysical" (p. 126). Instead, it can be viewed as a "constitutive aspect of the whole utterance, who under deeper analysis, can be revealed in it" (p. 127). In fact, this phenomenon in language that Bakhtin calls the "superaddressee" seems to stem from the dialogic "nature of the word, which always wants to be heard, always seeks responsive understanding, and does not stop at immediate understanding but presses on further and further (indefinitely)" (p. 127).

In her critique of "justice," Danielle sees justice not simply as an idea but as a term. Viewed under a Bakhtinian lens, Danielle is highlighting the social nature of language as a system of communication, used primarily in social settings to make sense of things (Fairclough, 2002; Filmer, 2003; Gee, 1989; Smitherman, 2006). We human beings, even when in total isolation, cannot help but project our language outside ourselves into a social setting, even if that setting happens to be absent at the time and space (Bakhtin, 1981; Derrida, 1967a). For us, this human tendency to project language outside ourselves is what gives rise to our stories, which we see as foundational points in the dialogic of theory and practice—in the promises of meaning.

In pursuit of meaning, Danielle continues her critique of the term *justice*. "It's funny," she says. "I can't understand what social justice teaching means without looking inside of me. Still, I can't be a social justice teacher without looking outside of me too." As Danielle begins to uncover quiet tensions in meaning, she unconsciously unfolds space (inner and outer space), the *heteroglossic* locations at which any dialogue occurs. Only then is she capable of defining the boundaries of justice. Still we wondered together, what occupies the space within her and between us? What lives in her and beyond us, capable of fostering complicated meanings and conditional/contradicting acts or practices? As our utilitarian needs become usurped and destabilized, teachers must utilize other spaces, "fourthspace" for example (see introduction), as a heterotopia so they can reconsider, reflect on, and rejuvenate meaning and a meaningful teaching practice. We are left to reason that teaching in space like teaching for justice means little outside the individuals who occupy spaces and terms. Hence, in binding meaning, we conclude that individuals unconsciously negotiate spaces—both inner, outer, and fourth spaces—in the process of brokering realities and acts (Bakhtin, 1984, 1986).

Before actions, then, there are questions. We continue our dialogue, pushing the Bakhtinian idea of dialogue to its limits. For Danielle, what does justice mean not simply in name, but also in deed? For both of us, how could one arrange an idea between spaces, where competing notions of a singular idea converge and compete? In the service of students, how does one bring harmony to an idea, which seems to deftly flee space and definition? Finally, how can one hear more clearly the voices within to make better sense of the outer voices in which ideas and acts are partially based?

To address these questions, Danielle and I reflect "inside-out" in conversation on both the inner and outer voices that shaped the stories that influenced Danielle's understanding of justice. Danielle's story about how she arrived at teaching gave me a glimpse into the process of understanding an idea—or in the Bakhtinian sense, "the process of ideological becoming" (Morson, 2004). As members of the dialogue, Danielle and I both are present in her story. Since it is difficult for us to define what it is that we do or where we are as social justice teachers, for on any given day and within any given situation our actions and locations may change—and that rather abruptly; we hope to open at least one of our souls and pour out our contemplations on our deepest commitments to justice. Perhaps our commitments to justice are so profound that to understand them would mean unfathomable reflection and unsounded struggle, a dialogic exercise undertaken to quiet the tensions we find in meaning. Recognizing the presence of great power in her story, Danielle summons the voice within her to share with me her process of making sense of social justice teaching. It moves in dialogue with a narrative stride that storytellers today imitate. Her story gives both "the word and the world" new meaning.

"Teaching Found Me": Making Sense of Justice from a Voice Within

I will never forget the day that I made the biggest decision of my life. I was in deep thought concerning my major and what I wanted to pursue as a career. I had entered college as a telecommunications major, hoping to become a disc jockey when I graduated. I had also considered journalism, as I really enjoyed writing and interacting with people.

Something though, on this particular day, spoke to my heart. A question caught me by surprise and actually overwhelmed me. As I walked across campus toward the building where I was supposed to meet with my advisor about changing my major, my heart asked me, "What can you do, Danielle, to really impact people?"

And I suppose I could have thought about that question for days, as there are many different answers. But my answer came instantly. I wanted to teach. And teaching English, for me, seemed to be the best way, I thought, to reach teenagers. We could read about life, write about life, talk about life. This is what went through my mind. The possibility of helping children connect to each other and to the limitless possibility within themselves drew me into the career. I didn't find teaching. Teaching found me.

There are no stops in Danielle's eyes. She looks solemn and serene as she gives voice to her memories. She is resolving the tensions in the meaning of a word, hoping to answer a question not easily answered. Danielle's attempt to resolve the tensions in meaning, to define for herself justice, starts with a voice—a voice from within. An internal dialogue, in which her heart gains voice, is present in our conversation. Her definition of social justice teaching, one could argue, began to emerge in that inner conversation well before she decided to "go into teaching," well before she decided to share her story with me. She informs me, "My ministry began this day."

For a social justice teacher trying to understand what it means to teach for social justice, how does one separate what is peculiar to memory, to personal struggle, to one's own situation which marks one's growing experience with epic stories about belonging and wanting to belong? What actually counts as social justice teaching, and what is only make-believe?

If we want to learn to untie the threads that weave together the idea of justice in her, whether loose or tight, we would have to begin from somewhere within Danielle. It is the only way that we can make sense of her inner voice, which speaks of "impacting people." We translate its message in our own hearts, which could be deceptive because hearts, while they are made to beat, do not always beat in unison and do not always obey reason. So we imagine. Perhaps Danielle had a trying childhood, where she was always responsible for helping others. Maybe her parents raised her to be benevolent, to look to the needs of others as if they were her own. Or perhaps she feels guilty and became obsessed with the possibility of redemption by dedicating herself to a "just" cause. Many of us teach for justice, but the reasons why and the ways we teach for justice may differ remarkably (Ayers et al., 1998; Kohl, 2000).

To be a woman draped in the company of gross inequities seemed like reason enough for Danielle to commit herself to social justice teaching. She could not have been the lone idealist who gave up everything—a dream in journalism and the awards it would have afforded—to embrace a mission to make a difference through a profession that many regard with contempt. Women even in this dynamic age rarely get to choose (Kristeva, 1986, 1991). The message that she gets from her heart must have surprised Danielle—terrified her. We will not lapse into extended conversation on Danielle's internal strivings. As a listener, they are mostly unknown to me. However, it is important to point out that Danielle honored her inner voice. She struggled at first with her decision to teach. Then she concluded that teaching was a site of struggle where she could make a difference. But struggle was all too familiar to Danielle. For according to her, "I've been a fighter since I can remember." She explains:

> I get that from my Daddy. He always taught me to stand up for what was right and to never, ever be afraid to be myself. His words were my shield, and I somehow managed to believe and act like I was some superhero. Whether I was confronting the bullies who picked on the little guy at school or getting in somebody's face for carelessly spewing out racist remarks, I was at the center of something always.
>
> One time I got suspended in eighth grade for a verbal argument I had gotten into with another student concerning [homeless people] on the street and our mistreatment of them. In high school, for mock elections, I was voted "Most Likely to Become the Mayor of Detroit." I was always defending something or someone. I don't know why I didn't just shut my big mouth or keep my thoughts and opinions to myself. I can only conclude that doing what I felt was right and fighting hard for it became and remained a priority for me. It was a central part of who I was, and who I would become.
>
> At MSU, I remained a fighter. But a confused one initially. This was ground I wasn't used to navigating. Here I was, in a sea of White female faces, feeling so very alone. Yes, I am White and female. I've got the same racial and gender make-up of about 80 percent of teachers in America, but, well, I'm gonna say it...I just wasn't white enough!
>
> I remember the discussions [in my teacher education classes] initiated by professors and TAs concerning white privilege, diversity, multiculturalism, equality, equity and all of the wonderful little concepts that they were supposed to incorporate into the class to say they addressed the needs of everyone. My critical response was always, "Is it really that hard to see that we do have White privilege?"
>
> I was always inquisitive. My questions and perspectives were different. I remember the looks from my peers. In some classes, there seemed to be a resounding accusation in their eyes: "whose side are you really on?" "'I'm on humanity's side, ya'll," my heart would strike back. "Just 'cause I'm hummin' a Jill Scott song or got my Tigers's cap tipped to the back or gotta little soul in my voice doesn't make me less White or more Black." I'm just me.

The voice from within Danielle is extravagant. Could she convince herself of things, define a world and its worth, and then live outside of it? We thought. For individuals who decided to heed the voice from within and live inside the world it creates, embracing struggle and fighting to change it, solace is never certain, especially when the inner voice and outer voices clash. The outer voice is not, after all, much different from the inner voice. They both give orders. They both seek to define things.

For Danielle, the orders, the definitions of why we teach—although dialogized—were not politically innocent. Each voice as it extended outwardly into space was saturated, perhaps oversaturated, with the intentions of others. Danielle might have separated the outer voices from her inner voice if only she did not question meaning. Like her inner voice, the outer voices raged within her. These voices did not fade quietly away from her but vociferously crept closer to her, prompting her to question meaning in tension. Her story evolved, sometimes as response to the other voices.

The Other Voices: "Encourage and Feed Me"

I saw something inherently wrong in the whole way that education was being presented to students. It did not take into account what lies at the center of people's hearts. Their experiences. Their struggles. Their voices. Education was a script written by people who did not care about the kids I wanted to teach. And nobody questioned this.

Of course, this was a big problem for me. The preservation of institutionalized racism at MSU, one of the "best" education programs in the country, was an even more enraging idea, an idea that I refused to chew up and digest. I spit it right back out and was either met by silence or an occasional argument. A strong statement to make.

As Danielle continues her story, the dialogue subtly shifts from a conversation in dialogue with a present inner voice to a conversation in dialogue with a present outer one. In a commensal tradition, where sound is precious, the powerful presences of the other voices quiet Danielle's internal discussion about her personal beliefs and feelings. A new discussion emerges about an outward reality that does not correspond with Danielle's inner voice. Her inner voice did not disappear, however. It was made to wait its turn. It, like Danielle, responded to this outer voice, which was characterized with confliction and scattered ideas. Danielle spoke of this outer voice, this authoritative discourse, as if it were omnipotent. It may have been authoritative and all knowing; however, the outer voice seemed unclear of what it actually knew. Nonetheless, Danielle quiets her inner voice and listens to what the outer voices have to say.

I just listen. I know what I went through as a child. It is part of the reason why I teach, but other people, when they tell their stories, it's a completely different deal. For example, one of my classmates told me that critical pedagogy was bullshit and that we hurt students by talking about oppression and power. I wanted to cuss her out, but I had to listen. As I listened to her, I could interpret what she was saying. I didn't agree with her, but her point was that justice had to do with helping students be successful in school as opposed to being critical of school.

The work of listening to outer voices demands that the feelings playing about in one's gut be momentarily silenced. Danielle, listening, allows the promising instructions from within to fall quiet like night cast over evening. For a moment, she lets dreams go and allows another voice to take over. She listens.

Both her and the voice from within her. Listening, Danielle hears her story, which desire freedom, penetrate from within her, branching into the voices of many others. All of the voices do not agree, but Danielle is able to situate hers alongside other voices that make similar and complementary sounds.

To sustain her story, she would have to continue to struggle. Danielle remembers, "I had to fight for my placement in Detroit. You helped get me in. My best friend and I were the only two people who I met in my 5 years of education courses at MSU [who] actually wanted to teach in Detroit City."

In her attempt to define justice, to recall why she decided to teach, her attention shifts intermittently from her personal struggles to my help getting her into her teaching placement to her best friend's company. More attention to others—other people, other places, other things. This gave Danielle's story new depth. In reconciling the many voices, we together wondered if Danielle would find the meaning she sought. If that meaning was about process (i.e., what does it mean to teach for justice), then it was also about identity (i.e., what does it mean to be a social justice teacher).

Together, Danielle and I learned from her story that she has had a mixed experience in her teacher education program. Her program sent her competing messages. There were voices that prepared her for social justice teaching, but there were also voices that did not.

"The curriculum, up until my senior year, did not prepare me, support me, or encourage me to teach in an urban environment," Danielle complains. "There were few students of color in my education courses, and they were, many times, questioned about the 'urban' perspective when and if it ever came up, as though their individual perspective was to represent an entire group of people."

As she continues her story, we began to realize that the meaning of justice for Danielle became tense. This tension, for Danielle, eluded control so stubbornly that a whole conversation was required to stave off the chaos of climatic noise (Derrida, 1982; Kristeva, 1991). However to fall completely silent would make meaning disappear, for there is no meaning without noise (Derrida, 1967b). A thing becomes what it is or what it will be when it simultaneously becomes everything that it is not. Tensions in meaning, appearances of things that did not match and Danielle's skepticism of mix-matching produced more questions. These questions promised to unite the disparate voices that churned chaotically within her.

The continuing dialogue of questions is where Danielle's inner voice is put into conversation with the outer voices. They do not come together out of sync. It is in dialogic unity that voices shimmer in the possibilities of meaning, balanced and held together in symmetry by space and interest. Things do not always fall apart. They sometimes come together. In this way, Danielle reasons, "I don't doubt that my TAs and peers meant well. We all wanted to serve in some way. If something did not appear to be broken, who would try to fix it? The system that served most of my peers worked quite well for them, so why would they see a need for change? Maybe they just couldn't see how broken it really was. I did."

With space to reflect on the quiet tensions in meaning, Danielle is beginning to understand what social justice teaching means—at least to her. Its meaning is not found in understanding her story alone. Danielle also sees a need to consider the stories of others in order to understand certain concepts like justice expressed in her own story. She must situate the histories, which surface in all voices. But she too has a story, which helps her to make sense of not only justice, but also the other voices. Danielle recalls attending Detroit Public Schools through eighth grade before her parents moved her out to a local suburb for her high school years. She explains:

> I saw the difference. And as we wrote one reflection paper after another at MSU, I began to get my arms around what informed my critical perspective. MSU, I will say, taught me how to reflect upon who I was, and what experiences helped to mold my pedagogy. I learned to hear my inner voice and how to question myself to find answers. This was an invaluable tool that I thank my program for providing. I just wish they would have provided more support for teachers who wanted to teach for justice in urban areas. Quite frankly, most of us didn't know what the hell justice meant. I wished that my teacher education would have prepared me to define justice so that I didn't have to tuck my education so neatly into a 'white' box.

Unlike the box that Ruth Vinz refers to in her foreword, the box that Danielle is referring to is completely metaphorical. It represents a place of dissension for Danielle, where she guards her secrets. Flayed, unprotected against space, she felt discomfort in not knowing. This ignorance quieted her; only in conversation would she dare to question what social justice teaching meant. However, in conversation there is hint that she suspected things about its meaning, as if she and it had somehow, long ago, been acquainted. The fallout was massive, though. She insisted on it in her teaching space. In her classroom, where all meanings are contested, it betrayed her, becoming something else, belonging to someone else. Nonetheless, she held onto what it once was and her fond memories of it. She kept them tucked away neatly in a "white box."

It is only in the conversation that she retrieves her secrets from the box. She realizes that at some point during her preservice teacher education, she knew what teaching for social justice meant. To help her explain, she remembers other voices. These are more familiar to her.

> My senior year at MSU, I met some amazing individuals who helped to encourage and feed me. I met Leah Kirell, a strong-minded individual who was upfront and honest, talented, who helped me to really understand the process behind actually 'teaching for social justice.' What sticks out the most in my mind concerning her was her 'tough-as-nails' demeanor and her narratives about teaching in D.C.
>
> I respected her. I respected where she came from and what she was trying to do. And most of all, I respected her high expectations of us. She didn't play. She kept it real. And she wasn't like anyone I had encountered previously in my education courses.

There was also Ernest Morrell. Ernest opened my eyes to critical theory in the classroom. I learned from him a language, essentially, a way to talk about literature in new ways and to empower youth by beginning with them first. What he implied, in his lessons, really pushed the envelope, went against the grain, but his delivery and his rationale were strong. I knew that what he was pushing us toward was exactly where I wanted to go, but I knew that I would have to learn how to defend myself. I knew that in taking any kind of risks, I needed to know the why and the how and the so what?

Ernest made sure we could always provide a rationale for everything we did. Despite having a big mouth, there were ideas and thoughts that I kept to myself, writing them off as abstract and too 'radical.' But Ernest made the impossible seem possible. We just had to believe in what we were trying to do and make sure we were able to articulate our ideas clearly and with good defense.

Danielle may have reached into her "white box" to convince herself that justice still had meaning. Reaching back into the box also shows concern over its meaning. Otherwise leave it closed.

Danielle confesses,

Much of teaching, I believe, has to do with love and community and fostering this in children. I think that professors and programs sometimes forget this. In Leah, Ernest, and later you, I heard narratives that encouraged my emerging sense of social justice. From them, I heard stories that reflected love. Love sparked my interest. The voices of others somehow showed me how to meet children where they were at the beginning with their voices and their experiences.

These professionals touched my heart with their stories and helped me to realize how important it was to show my students how much they had to offer their communities, their families, and us. We just had to listen to them and help them to develop their own critical perspective and a language to talk about that perspective.

Finding Meaning in Tension: An Ongoing Dialogue

The conversation continued for hours. From it, we moved closer to consensus that justice has a definite meaning although we were not sure of it. In spite of our uncertainty, Danielle's story was helping us to discover it. Prior to teaching, Danielle was perhaps more certain about what justice meant. Having taught in and experienced education in Detroit, I was more certain of what it was not.

In many preservice teacher education program across the nation, justice, as a fashionable catch term, has been romanticized and reduced, not often associated with teachers helping students pass standardized tests. In these early years of teacher education, teachers like Danielle defined justice from their dreams. But as they transition from preservice to inservice spaces, teachers including Danielle become pressured to define justice from their and their students' realities, especially as those realities increasingly become measured by high-stakes tests.

If Danielle had chosen to teach in another community, where more students achieved academic success and new, vogue traditions were typically permitted, perhaps she might have held on to what, in college, she believed justice to mean. But in Detroit, students were sometimes quite literally being left behind or altogether forced out of education. Being average for the majority of her students meant failing. The district and her students' parents, desperate for solutions, synced their ideas of justice to standardization, to teaching that could raise students' test scores, and to teachers who could be held accountable to existing standards.

Danielle was a fighter. She did not easily buy into the district's or her student's parents definitions of justice. She, remembering that "women give birth through labor," struggled instead for meaning. She explains,

> This is where hip-hop comes in. It became like a secret underground movement that my students and I would be a part of to arrive at, through the back door, the curriculum demands of the school. With no exception, every single time I developed a lesson or conversation that referenced hip-hop or used hip-hop as a central focus, my students, each and every one of them, were attentive and engaged.
>
> Hip-hop's power is no secret. It is just as rich of a text as any piece of Western canonical literature. We've just got to create enough space in our classrooms to explore it and use it in effective ways.

Danielle, subject to multiple pulls from the voices that existed both inside and outside her, struggled to make justice as meaningful in practice as in theory. In theory, there was place for popular culture in her classroom. But when theory did not translate, into test scores, there was a tension with practice. However, she began to understand that if the meaning of justice was to be authentic outside her, justice had to resolve competing interests and competing notions of what it could be within her. In the interests of multiple players, justice could mean essentially anything in any given moment. Yet for Danielle, the meaning of justice had to serve her students and not simply her district. She acknowledged the multiple sets of voices—from within and those from without—and somehow sanctioned a new becoming that could quiet the tensions in meaning. But when silence fell, the meanings of justice that Danielle sanctioned drew farther apart. A new space was needed in which to define not just the term but also the process. This space did not exist within Danielle's school, her university classrooms, or within her. It existed within her students, who like all the other spaces mentioned existed within her.

As such, Danielle brokered meaning by negotiating spaces—bringing her students worlds in contact with her tensions. According to Danielle, "Sometimes I would reference a quote from Tupac or Nas to start off a class just to get the students' attention, and then move into a lesson that built upon the concept mentioned in the quote."

She explained,

We would dissect one line from a Pac song, 'Some say the darker the berry, the sweeter the juice, I say the darker the flesh then the deeper the roots…', talking about the significance of such a comparison, stereotypes based upon 'blackness,' and pride rooted in one's history. We would talk and write until the bell rang…and I had to ask them to leave!

On two separate occasions, I have taught Othello and have seen my students produce modern-day hip-hop versions of the play. The last occasion involved middle school students who were initially scared to death of Shakespeare. Once they realized that their lives were full of Othellos, Desdemonas, Iagos, Emilias, and Roderigos, they jumped right in. I just had to start with them.

While she found that the definition of justice resided in multiple spaces, Danielle understood the question implicit in defining justice. The quiet tension found in the meaning of justice was instigated in that question. That is, justice *for* whom? While justice *to* Danielle and to those forces that influenced her matter, Danielle's story illustrates that, in defining justice, teachers comment on who they serve. In process, they are answering the question for whom. However, in practice, they experience continuing doubt. Even in service of students, social justice teachers may still feel an ever-present tension:

I will admit that although I use hip-hop often, I still believe I could do more. In my current position, my 6th graders and I reference pop culture all of the time. In fact, my students now teach me: 'Ms. Filipiak, I think I know what u sayin' about tone…like Beyonce was really feelin' alone in that song even though the song's theme was about love. So the tone would be loneliness, I think.' I have to make tradeoffs. My reply, 'Yeah, I think you are onto something. Her song is a text. These books we are reading are texts. So, think of it this way, when you are reading your books, how do you think your author is feeling? You figured out how to 'read' that song, now just use the same technique with your book. How was the author feeling while he/she was writing?'

Key to Danielle was how she positioned her students in her definitions of social justice. With her students in mind, justice was an ongoing process of making "tradeoffs," helping youth—like Dewey said—learn how to think for themselves:

See, my kids get it. Most of our kids get it. They just have a different way of looking at text. Their lives are saturated with certain kinds of texts. Many of them have to stay indoors because they aren't allowed to go outside. Their neighborhoods are not safe enough. So iPods, TVs, and video games become their sidekicks. They 'read' these all of the time. So when I reference these texts, I am telling them, in a way, that they are okay. That what they read and see is not of any less worth than Beowulf or To Kill a Mockingbird or 'The Road Not Taken.'

Still not statisfied, Danielle concedes, "But, as I said before, I believe I could do more. This still is not enough."

For justice to achieve meaning for Danielle, the conversation has to continue. She must continuously struggle with the quiet tensions in meaning. Her story must continue:

> All of this seems to make sense. At least to me it does. But to some parents and administrators, it doesn't. And I am always playing the role of negotiator. I feel as though I am constantly trying to cut a deal with someone. And because of this, I have felt that I just can't take what I believe in too far. Yet. What is too far? Well, what would happen if we started seeing politically-minded songs by Public Enemy or NWA in a textbook? Or used Shakespeare to teach Tupac instead of Tupac to teach Shakespeare? Why do we insist on treating our students' texts as platforms to understand 'real' texts rather than treating their texts as valid knowledge? This does not feel like justice to me. This is why I say that we just aren't doing enough. I'm not doing enough.
>
> I'm still trying to figure out how to make this work. See, when I talk about my theories with some parents or administrators, they express assumptions, like maybe I am lowering my expectations of students, treating them like they aren't smart enough to handle what they 'should' be learning. Or maybe my kids are talking about stuff that is inappropriate. So what do I do when I get called down to the office? Or get that phone call from a parent who is enraged about a conversation her child had with others in my classroom? How far is too far?
>
> See, I am a young White face. Blue eyes, long hair. I am going to touch on this because I think that it is significant. We don't talk about it, but it is out there. I'm young, don't have many years under my belt, and care deeply about my kids. I get a parent coming at me and saying, 'I don't need some White woman telling my child what to do. You don't know what these kids need.' Wow. Strike to the heart. Or from a principal, 'Here at School X, we have a certain way of teaching and specific expectations that enable our students to be prepared for college. What you are doing is stuff that just doesn't fit in to what we believe is best for students at our school.'
>
> How does one disarm these individuals? Well, some just cannot be disarmed. And I have learned this. However, when we care as much as we do, sometimes it is difficult not to take things personally and get fired up. Regardless of this, I feel that it is important to disarm with two things 1. Love and 2. Truth.
>
> With administrators, most of the time, I find it best to defend myself once with examples and quotes and numbers (Truth in objective format). After that, I just close my door. I find that they leave you alone when they observe higher test scores and students who respect you without yelling. And if they don't, well, I don't let fear motivate my teaching.
>
> I let my heart guide everything. And if I become a bit shaken up by a critical conversation with someone higher up or a parent, I reflect, maybe vent with the 1 or 2 colleagues, if any, that I can trust, and then I move on. I just remind myself to not hold back simply because I am scared. Eventually, if they want to get rid of me- then so be it. I believe too much in what I am trying to do to give my students less than they deserve.
>
> With my parents, I provide as much love as possible. Parents know when you love their children. I speak honestly with parents, and begin and end every conversation with something positive. There is always something positive to find about a child. Some people might say, 'oh, but you must not know about the devil child I have in my classroom…' There is always at least one student who gets on his/her teacher's last nerve. But there is something that makes that child special, or brilliant, or brave, or in-

telligent. I think that starting with these attributes is beneficial. Okay. Enough about that. The point is that every teacher needs to be armed with weapons of the heart (love and truth, for me), in attempts to connect what he/she is doing to the agendas that parents and administrators have.

Danielle saw a need to bring harmony to the many voices that influenced her teaching. In doing so, she is asking, does justice act in the service of everyone at once or no one at all? The question is profound, as justice is too often defined in tangents and extremes. Too often we mistake its dialogics for debate.

Does an ongoing dialogue mean that social justice teachers must abandon our personal teaching agenda? Perhaps, the opposite is true; social justice teachers must fully embrace it. In embracing it, social justice teachers must also fully understand it and continuously struggle to make sense of it. In her journey into social justice teaching, Danielle is in process. This process of defining social justice for her has three prongs:

1. Realization: embracing who I am and why I teach;
2. Explanation: understanding what it means to be a social justice teacher, how one teaches for social justice, and how to explain that to others;
3. Action: teaching for social justice, taking into account what it means or may mean in a given situation.

This process is illustrated in Danielle's story, which by now is coming close to an end. She is clearer about what social justice means to her. She is also clearer about the agenda that she embraces in her teaching.

The agenda that I have in the center of my heart remains social activism. What a term, 'social activism.' What does that mean? What does that look like? Why is it so important to me and why do I believe it is so important for my students? Well, where my students come from, change must come. I just don't see it in any other way. And I, we, must take action to see that change comes.

Enough of the obvious. What are we really doing to help our children—choking them with an agenda that has nothing to do with them so that the current structures in society remain the same while keeping my students and their families last in line? Somebody must do something to keep this from continuing to happen, to break these trends. And here is where justice comes in. Here is why the idea is so important. It has the tremendous ability, within our classrooms, to help our students see themselves as agents of change.

We cannot do this, however, by talking to them about change or allowing our expectations of them to rely upon their success in mastering concepts or ways of thinking that mean nothing to them. I used hip-hop to value their literacies and experiences, which for me was of the utmost importance. We need to think of new ways of social justice teaching to allow urban kids to thrive, to feel successful. We need to be comfortable enough with ourselves to give them that kind of space.

Look at it this way, it can't get much worse. Our children, within urban districts, are failing tests at astronomical rates. Dropout rates are tremendous at the high school level. Even at the college level. How much longer are we just going to stand here and watch this happen? When we begin to employ techniques that validate our children, welcome them, show them that success if possible, we will see changes. Our children will become social activists themselves. They will find new ways to change what they see, but on top of putting their voices and experiences at the center of our curriculums, we must provide new experiences for them.

When Danielle is done telling her story, my definition of social justice becomes clearer as well. I learn that social justice teaching implies a forward movement in both meaning and in action. Hence, social justice teachers fail if our only goal is to leave no child behind. It seems an awkward goal to me. However, many of you dear readers might be wondering, what is awkward about "leaving no child behind?" The slogan, to Danielle and I, feels sadly defeatist, as if we have chosen not to march forward to compel new meanings, to quiet the tension within, and to lead our children ahead. We know that as long as the conversation continues, there will be hope. And as Timothy Lensmire (2000) reminds us, hope is the project we retain so that our students can "imagine new roles and lives for themselves in our society" (p. 6).

Becoming a Social Justice Teacher

Frozen in Danielle's story are voices arranged in quiet tension that flee basic meaning. We are both beset within them, traveling through random mounds of tension, to decipher the many channels of meaning. Hence, our understandings of justice are located in history, affixed to the extremes of power, but more importantly they emanate from specific locales of stories—both ours and others. They position us and are positioned within us, as we position them too. But here we have appropriated a larger cause: to educate youth. To accomplish our agenda, we look back on our own stories—the ones that we have put in conversation with our students stories to understand how this might be done.

Common to Danielle's story, my story, and the stories of many others are themes of passion and pain. It is unclear to me which theme comes first. However, it does seem clear to me that pain defines social injustice, as passion may define a reaction against it. Without a clear understanding of what is unjust, however, one cannot truly define what is just. Hence, if social injustice is associated with pain, then social justice—in opposing it—must deal with the passion in healing both as an act and as a process. One aspect of social justice teaching must then be an act of healing, internally and externally, the pain that each of us uniquely and collectively witnesses and experiences. Social justice teaching seems to acknowledge a responsibility to others. "(Inter)acting justly," North (2006) writes, "then, requires a consideration of the others that we encounter and have already encountered, in lived experiences or history, for the fuller realization of our mutually constituted selves requires that we speak *and* listen" (p. 526, emphasis in original).

From this perspective, meaning flows through, but not just within a word. It clears our experiences where words give way to quiet streams of meaning diverging sideways, winding, and sometimes colliding with competing ideologies. This tension is alive in Danielle as it is in me. Perplexed. Meaning exists only as we make it mean, only as we make sense of the tensions found in words, and as we understand truly our causes. In this way, Gumperz and Hymes (1972) found the study of language a complex affair. For Gumperz and Hymes, "meanings may be won by the sweat of the brow, and communication is achieved in labor" (p. 272).

Hence, social justice is meaningless unless we make it mean. And what we make of it differs with respect to time and space. It varies by situation and is transmogrified in space. Theresa Rogers, Elisabeth Marshall, and Cynthia Tyson (2006) make this point clear when they argue "that because schools are riddled with inequities, they are limited spaces in which new teachers can expect to confront their own prejudices and privilege and to learn about issues of diversity and social justice . . ." (p. 221).

While every statement is inextricably bound to the context in which it exists, it is too embodied in individuals and in individuals' stories. A conversation of meaning that emanates from the teacher narrative promises to diminish the distance separating teachers' preservice and inservice experiences. Rogers et al. (2006) believe

> Practices such as creating spaces for dialogue in which complex issues can be raised have the potential to help students teachers to broaden their own and their peers' social and cultural perspectives beyond simplified narratives about education. We also see the dialogic narratives of preservice teachers as central to our understanding of how mediated community-based learning experiences may explain how prospective teachers begin to construct their professional identities in terms of their beliefs about language and diversity in and out of schools and the strategies they develop for connecting to their students' families and communities. (p. 221)

Hence, the pedagogical issue of social justice teaching is an issue of how one appropriates the concept and binds meaning within it. It is never nebulous, but tenuous—an issue of meaning. For some, the definition of justice resides in the individual or in the flexibility of the form or the utterance. Others argue that justice means nothing at all, for the very concept is wrought with perplexity and split in ambiguity. Therefore, it fails to achieve that to which it sanctions, and fails to define that to which it attempts to move forward.

In a fine Bakhtinian sense, however, the meaning of justice exists as it were on the fringes of dialogue. As it seems, the major contribution of this work is to inspire conversations about how people experience justice—about how they participate in it to create it to call it into being. That is, how do our stories contribute to meaning? We assume that the writers of *NCLB* legislation were voicing their visions of social justice. It is highly probable that *NCLB* was conceived as a proclamation of our nation's commitment to all children. It was a voice that verged in the direction of freedom even while it was a different vision of justice than what many of us perceive justice to be.

What happens when meanings fail to match? Is anyone heard? Do students, the ones who need us most, benefit? These questions begin to shape our sense of justice. While Danielle's story has helped us, it goes beyond testimonial. Her personal story gives us one significant response in an ongoing dialogue on justice. It is not meant to be a dictate. Rather, it has been meant to bring forth the voices that occupy spaces, a classroom or a page—it doesn't matter—which sanction meanings enacted in practices like teaching. What is left is a tangible, knowable artifact, well told, stained with the impressions of some of our greatest educational challenges, questions, and primary means for understanding one another. By thinking hard about these challenges, questions, and means, by looking hard at the stories which define them, something strangely magical, something surprisingly meaningful emerges. We learn, not just about how to teach, but also about how to occupy our teaching spaces. We learn how to heal.

It is a wonder that Danielle believes:

> That within people exists an innate desire to love and to feel loved. To contribute to something larger then themselves, even if in a small way. Sometimes this may become clouded by experiences or bitterness or rejection or all of the many things that make us so beautifully human. We forget though, in our everyday lives, to stop and listen. To return back to the fabric of who we are and what we so desperately desire. To love others and to allow others to love us.

References

Ayers, W., Hunt, J. A., & Quinn, T. (Eds.). (1998). *Teaching for social justice: A democracy and education reader.* New York, NY: New Press.

Bakhtin, M. M. (1981). *The dialogic imagination: Four essays* (M. Holquist & C. Emerson, Trans.). Austin: University of Texas Press.

———. (1984). *Problems of Dostoevsky's poetics* (C. Emerson, Trans.). Minneapolis: University of Minnesota Press.

———. (1986). *Speech genres and other late essays.* Austin: University of Texas Press.

Cochran-Smith, M., Davis, D., & Fries, K. (2003). Multicultural teacher education research, policy, and practice. In J. A. Banks (Ed.), *The Handbook of research on multicultural education* (2nd ed.). San Francisco: Jossey-Bass.

Derrida, J. (1967a). *Of grammatology* (G. C. Spivak, Trans.). London: Johns Hopkins University Press.

———. (1967b). *Writing and difference* (A. Bass, Trans.). Chicago: University of Chicago Press.

———. (1982). *Margins of philosophy.* Chicago: University of Chicago Press.

Fairclough, N. (2002). *Language and power.* New York: Addison Wesley Longman.

Featherstone, J. (1989). To make the wounded whole. *Harvard Educational Review, 59*, 367-378.

Filmer, A. A. (2003). African-American Vernacular English: Ethics, ideology, and pedagogy in conflict between identity and power. *World Englishes, 22*(3), 253-270.

Gee, J. P. (1989). What is literacy? *Journal of Education, 171*(1), 5-25.

Greenleaf, C. L., & Katz, M.-L. (2004). Voices in dialogue—Multivoiced discourses in ideological becoming. In A. F. Ball & S. W. Freedman (Eds.), *Bakhtinian perspectives on language, literacy, and learning* (pp. 172-202). New York: Cambridge University Press.

Gumperz, J., & Hymes, D. (1972). *Directions in socio-linguistics: The ethnography of communication.* New York: Holt, Rinehart and Winston.

Kohl, H. (2000). Teaching for social justice. Retrieved January 21, 2007, from Rethinking Schools: http://www.rethinkingschools.org/archive/15_02/Just152.shtml.

Kristeva, J. (1986). Word, dialogue, and novel (A. Jardine, T. Gora, & L. S. Roudiez, Trans.). In T. Moi (Ed.), *The Kristeva reader* (pp. 34-61). New York: Columbia University Press.

———. (1991). *Strangers to ourselves.* New York: Columbia University Press.

Lensmire, T. (2000). *Powerful writing, responsible teaching.* New York: Teachers College Press.

Morson, G. S. (2004). The process of ideological becoming. In A. F. Ball & S. W. Freedman (Eds.), *Bakhtinian perspectives on language, literacy, and learning* (pp. 317-331). New York: Cambridge University Press.

North, C. E. (2006). More than words? Delving into the substantive meaning (s) of "social justice" in education. *Review of Educational Research, 76*(4), 507-535.

Pang, V. O., & Gibson, R. (2001). Concepts of democracy and citizenship: Views from African American teachers. *The Social Studies, 92*(6), 260-266.

Rogers, T., Marshall, E., & Tyson, C. A. (2006). Dialogic narratives of literacy, teaching, and schooling: Preparing literacy teachers for diverse settings. *Reading Research Quarterly, 41*(2), 202-224.

Smitherman, G. (2006). *Word from the mother: Language and African Americans.* New York: Routledge.

4

Dream Big: The Power of Literature, Imagination, and the Arts

Peggy Rice with Alena Bogucki, Jamey Katen, and Emily Marie Keifer

---

> We live our lives through texts. They may be read, or changed or experienced elec-
> tronically, or come to us, like the murmurings of our mothers, telling us what conven-
> tions demand. Whatever their form or medium, these stories have formed us all; they
> are what we must use to make new fictions, new narratives. (Heilbrun, 1988, p.37.)

Writing this narrative has been an insightful journey for me. Forty-plus years
living life, ten years teaching elementary students, eleven years teaching university students, and eleven years researching aspects of race, class and gender….numerous stories surfaced, seeking to be told, as I pondered the following questions: *When did I first become aware of my own social justice pedagogy? Why is a
social justice pedagogy important to me? How is social justice entwined in my pedagogy? Life?
How do I help English education students develop a critically conscious social justice pedagogy?
What are my concerns about its efficacy in the schools?* When I read Ruth's foreword, I
was reminded of Ramon.

I met Ramon when I was teaching third grade in El Paso, Texas, my third
year of teaching and my first year teaching ESL. Having grown up in the Mid-
west with a desire to travel to France, I had studied French as my foreign language rather than Spanish, so teaching a bilingual immersion class in El Paso,
Texas challenged my teaching practices. I began the year with nine students
whose understanding of the English language was emerging. Unable to communicate with them in Spanish and realizing that the third grade texts provided
for their instruction were beyond the students' language ability; I quickly turned
to children's literature (picture books) and the arts for instruction.

About a month after school started, the guidance counselor informed me
that I was getting a new student, Ramon, who would be with me until his IEP
meeting in a few weeks. *Ramon has limited English proficiency, is deaf and B.D. We are
putting him with you for the next few weeks, because no one else can control him.* I remember thinking to myself, "Now, this will be interesting." I wasn't quite sure what

to expect. I immediately told my students we would have a new member in our community and set about establishing him in our community. Later that day, the guidance counselor escorted Ramon to my room. The moment I saw him, my heart went out to him. Ramon was tiny, almost frail, had a mop of curly dark brown hair and an apprehensive look in his large brown eyes (he certainly didn't look uncontrollable). We welcomed him into our community. At first, he was reluctant and shy about participating. Like any learner, he needed to understand the learning situation/expectations in order to participate. His special needs exceeded those of my other students, so engaging him in learning activities was a challenging and daunting task, but I was determined. I continued with my focus on incorporating imagination and the arts with picture books. Ramon needed more modeling than the other students so I engaged them in the role of mentors. Within a couple of days, Ramon became a contributing member of our community and the apprehensive look in his eyes changed into an excited gleam. His presence empowered my other students as they took the position of mentors. I was excited and discussed his engagement with the school's administration in the hopes that he would be able to remain in my class and was told that I could express my views at his IEP meeting. The day of the IEP meeting arrived. Ramon's mother and a translator appeared in my door prior to the beginning of school. I was excited that his mother had noticed the difference in Ramon's attitude toward school and also wanted him to remain in my class. I was optimistic as I headed toward his IEP meeting shortly after the bell rang signaling the beginning of the school day. Unfortunately, the person scheduled to cover my class had arrived a few minutes late, so I was the last to arrive at the meeting. I remember my optimistic attitude waning as I entered the room. The meeting had begun without me and although the administrators paused to enable the school guidance counselor to introduce me to the two district administrators, they quickly resumed their discussion. As I listened, it became apparent that the administrators had already made a decision to move Ramon to a school within the district for hearing impaired children. Although his mother and I voiced our preferences that he remain in my class; our voices were not heard. I liken this incident to a comment Ruth shared in her introduction, "I did not know how to navigate or traverse all the streams of competing and conflicting values, beliefs and purposes." Ramon and I were "boxed into" social spaces within the educational system, Ramon had been labeled, and I had been silenced. Not only was Ramon removed from my classroom, but he was also removed from the school. I was disheartened and frustrated. Through the years, I have felt that I failed him. Unbeknownst to me at the time, I was embracing a social justice pedagogy, but unable to navigate the intransigent educational system. How do we attain social justice in teaching when institutional practices create barriers?

Professional organizations like NCTE provide dialogic spaces, such as the CEE Commission on Social Justice. The annual conference in Nashville, 2006 was especially beneficial for me in terms of developing understandings of uniting mind and body in order to more fully embody a critical pedagogy. When sj presented her theory of a loaded matrix in thirdspace as co-constructing the identity of the preservice teacher at our panel presentation, I began to think more critically about the co-construction of the identities of my preservice teachers and excitedly asked her to send me her paper. Our presentations, along with the conversations that took place during our CEE Commission on Social Justice meeting, which led to the creation of this book, rejuvenated me. While writing this chapter for the past several months, I have engaged in what sj calls the 5 "re-s" of "fourthspace": "reflect, reconsider, reconceptualize, rejuvenate and reengage." As I stated earlier, it has been an insightful journey.

Becoming Aware

A large part of who I am developed during a sheltered childhood in which I had very little actual power. I am a forty-plus White, liberal female who grew up on an approximately three hundred acre dairy farm in Illinois, the next to youngest of five girls. Our house was isolated (a quarter mile from the nearest road, a mile from the nearest neighbors and ten miles from the nearest town) and my parents had opted not to have a television or a telephone in the house. Our family structure was patriarchal; my dad ruled the house with an iron fist and the wrath of God (he was the Sunday School Superintendent at the Baptist Church we attended at least once per week). Children were to be seen and not heard. We were expected to "toe the line." The Ten Commandments were to be followed and the Golden Rule was stressed.

Education, especially the value of learning through reading, was emphasized by both of my parents. In addition to subscriptions to daily newspapers and monthly magazines, we traveled to the local library every Friday and each of us (including my parents) would check out an armful of books. Books empowered me. They enabled me to exit my powerless existence in first space (real and actual space) and enter second space (imagined space) (Soja, 1996). Because of this, our weekly visit to the library was extremely important to me. I would thoughtfully select my reading choices for the week. Where did I want to go? Who did I want to meet? What experiences did I want to have? I traveled to Holland and shared skating adventures with Hans and Gretel *(Hans Brinker* or the *Silver Skates)*; endured the Oklahoma Dust Bowl with Rosasharn and the rest of the Joads *(Grapes of Wrath)*; rejoiced in Wilbur and Charlotte's friendship *(Charlotte's Web)*; frolicked with Pippi Longstocking and her animals; solved mysteries with Nancy Drew; flew with Amelia Earheart; and, shot the walnut off of the tree with Annie Oakley. Living vicariously through the characters, I developed understandings of the world, such as "People experience all kinds of ups and downs in life, but everything always works out in the end," "Women can achieve greatness," "Good will overcome evil"; and, as a result of these understandings, my strong sense of justice developed.

However, for the most part, I was unaware of issues of race, class and gender and their impact upon people. I was living in an "all white world of children's literature" (Larrick, 1965). Unlike today, marginalized voices, such as relocated Native Americans, enslaved African Americans, imprisoned Asian Americans, were missing from the books of my youth. Although I was vaguely aware of the Civil Rights Movement, racism was a non-relevant concept for me. I lived in an all White world; at church, I learned that Jesus loved all of the little children of the world and developed the belief that I should not judge people. At school, the instructional practice of tracking/ability grouping and the predominantly functional literacy ideology framed my learning instruction. The focus of the instruction was on "skill and drill" rather than engaging in texts and stories critically or to critically examine the historical and lived contexts of students' lives. So, although I embodied a strong sense of justice, I also viewed the world through rose colored glasses.

It wasn't until I was a doctoral student enrolled in a course focusing on race, class, and gender in schooling that I became aware of my own social justice pedagogy. Before that class, I had not interrogated the way(s) my race, class and gender configure my identity and pedagogy. A powerful assignment for me was the autobiographical essay:

> In this five-page, double-spaced typewritten essay, you are to locate yourself with respect to gender, socio-economic class and race Who are you, from whence have you come, and how have these particular markers and experiences affected/shaped/constructed your identity(ies)? How has/have your identity(ies) changed or been transformed over the course of your life thus far? When we read this essay, we will be looking for your capacity to reflect critically on, reveal and even challenge the taken-for-granted assumptions and "common-sense" knowledge that you hold. We want you to connect your "personal" story with the social/economic/political/ historical/cultural milieus in which you are situated. In other words, we expect you to think "sociologically" as well as "psychologically" about who you are and your relation to the larger society and culture.

That assignment provided me with an opportunity to articulate who I am as a raced/classed/gendered person and develop understandings of the "whys" and "hows" of my identity positioning(s) in society and culture. Although I do not have a copy of this assignment, written about eleven years ago, I recall a great deal of reflection and writing as I pondered the following questions: Who am I? Why do I position myself this way? How has my identity been shaped by societal markers such as race, class and gender? I began to think critically about race, class and gender—the inequities in our society, my previous obliviousness to the inequities (due to the rose colored glasses of my sheltered childhood) and my vision for the future. A burning question for me was, "How can I address the –ISMS so that my students (preservice Elementary Education Majors) are able to develop a social justice pedagogy, in which all students are treated fairly and equitably?"

While reading *Releasing the Imagination* (Greene, 1995), I realized the importance of seeing things and people big:

> To see things or people big, one must resist viewing other human beings as mere objects or chess pieces and view them in their integrity and particularity instead. One must see from the point of view of the participant in the midst of what is happening if one is to be privy to the plans people make, the initiatives they take, the uncertainties they face. (p. 10)

I also realized that I needed to gain additional insights into issues of gender, class and race in education. Thus, my research agenda was created. The insights I have gained into issues of gender, race and class in education have informed my social justice pedagogy. Certain aspects are important to consider as we take into account the loaded matrix (Miller & Norris, 2007) and "thinking big" in order to move toward a more just social order.

Course and Collaborators

In 2001, I developed an undergraduate senior seminar focusing on the trends and issues in the teaching of elementary English language arts. One of my goals for the course has been to help my elementary education students with a concentration in the teaching of elementary English language arts develop a critically conscious social justice pedagogy. I have consistently made changes each time I have taught the course, so my collaborators did not have an identical experience; however, I have always structured the course to be student-centered and inquiry based with many opportunities for reflection as we consider best practice vs. common practice, especially in terms of implementing instruction that enables all of our students to meet the NCTE/IRA standards for English Language Arts. In addition, I have always emphasized the value of literature reflecting a diverse perspective in connection to topics such as censorship, critical literacy, reflection, and imagination and the arts as we consider developing a social justice pedagogy in which all of our students are treated fairly and equitably. Within these discussions, I emphasize the importance of establishing community and developing empathy.

My stories, the stories of my seminar students (especially student teaching stories), and the stories published in professional journals such as *Language Arts* provide a framework for the discussions that occur within our community. For instance, one of the first articles we read is Commeyras's (2002), "Provocative Questions that Animate My Thinking about Teaching. In this article, Commeyras reflects on her experiences as she asks and answers the following questions in order to better align her practices with her beliefs:

•Do I believe that as a teacher I am an intellectual?
•Do I believe that as a teacher I am political?
•Do I believe that society has made me something that I no longer want to be?
•Do I believe reading requires attending to the political, social, and historical context of a text?
•Do I believe education always presupposes a vision of the future?

Before we discuss this article, I ask the students to articulate their vision of the future, and what they plan to do as a teacher to promote that vision and ask why that is vision important to them? Our discussion consists of critical reflections of our experiences. Throughout the semester, as we *reflect* critically on our stories and the stories of others, we are able to *reconsider* and *reconceptualize*. *What would I do differently? How can I better align my practices with my beliefs? What insights can we gain from this story?* We think critically about common practice vs. best practice and my students develop an understanding that the IRA/NCTE Standards for the English Language Arts should frame their learning instruction. In doing so, they begin to develop a social justice pedagogy in which all of their students are treated fairly and equitably.

Collaborators

Jamey Katen was enrolled in the course during the fall of 2002 and graduated from Ball State University in 2003 with a degree in Elementary Education. She is entering her fifth year of teaching. Her first two years of teaching, she taught fourth grade in Calumet City, Illinois. For the past two years, she taught second grade at a small private school in Columbus, Ohio. She is beginning her fifth year teaching fourth grade in Raleigh, North Carolina. I invited her to collaborate because she expressed a deep interest in my research while a student in my class and had contacted me about it after her graduation; however, I had not worked closely with her as an inservice teacher developing her curriculum. The senior seminar enabled her to become aware of her own social justice pedagogy. She says:

I first became aware of teaching for social justice during an undergraduate course at Ball State University. The professor, Dr. Peggy Rice, introduced social justice in the course, ENG 401. This was a senior seminar course that required deep discussions of trends and issues in literacy education. Dr. Rice required us to read professional journal articles and read the book Trends & Issues in Elementary Language Arts, which taught me about new trends in teaching Language Arts. These were all great resources for pre-service teachers. I found the professional journal articles and the textbook for the course significant to pre-service teachers because we were able to learn about best practices in the classroom and discuss our views in a seminar course. In addition, Dr. Rice had high expectations for her students and required us to do a research project and lead our own discussion seminar with our class. Some of the other topics covered that helped me during my first year of teaching were writer's workshop, literature groups, intertextuality, quality children's literature reflecting a diverse perspective, critical literacy, choral reading, and readers' theatre.

Emily Marie Keifer was enrolled in the course during the spring of 2007. She graduated from Ball State University in May 2007 and is preparing for her first year of teaching. She has accepted a position teaching fifth and sixth grade reading at a small rural school district in the area. ENG 401 also enabled her to become aware of her own social justice pedagogy. Emily speaks:

> Eng 401 developed my social justice pedagogy through two types of information gathering: Readings and group discussions. It was very helpful to me to hear about experiences that others had while dealing with the teaching of social justice through literature. Before 401 I was not aware of ways to teach about social justice within the classroom. There are so many topics that can be brought up in the classroom (socio-economic and racial especially) through literature. Before 401, I had the mindset that when thinking about these topics it was best to avoid teaching them due to concerns brought on by parents. During 401 I was able to hear a variety of voices concerning the teaching of these subjects. By reflecting on these readings and discussions, I was able to create my own views on the ways to use these types of literature and the ways that they are beneficial to the students.

Alena Bogucki, is a recent graduate of Ball State University, but not one of my former students. She earned a BS in Secondary Education at Ball State University in May of 2006. I met her at the summer meeting of *Women in Literacy and Life Assembly (WILLA)* this past summer. She had just completed her first year of teaching in which she taught ninth and tenth grade honors English. Although she first became aware of her own social justice pedagogy the summer prior to her first year of teaching, several of her professors influenced her during her undergraduate preparation. Alena tells us:

> One July evening, about a month before beginning my first year of teaching, my fiancée and I sat down to eat dinner in the living room of the house he shared with five of his friends. With plates balanced on our knees, a documentary on the Discovery Channel soon stole my appetite while filling me with thought and admitted anxiety. Chronicling the near-future consequences of continued global warming,–melting of the polar ice caps, rising ocean levels while diluting saline concentrations, and the extinction of hundreds of species–the hour-long show truly immersed me in a dire picture. After unplugging the TV and turning off all the lights in the house to limit CO_2 emissions, I realized

that in three weeks I would have a hundred people "at my disposal" to help. I had hope due to several of my former professors.

One of the major influences and individuals in my maturation from one possessing a high school mentality to somebody capable of successfully leading and facilitating experiences for high schoolers, was definitely the professor who facilitated my initial teacher education class, which I took during the fall semester of my freshman year in college. Throughout the entire course, whether discussing the waves of educational reform since the beginning of public education, or thinking back on my own experiences as a middle and high school student to compose INTASC principle analyses, reflection was the core component that made the content of that class meaningful to me. The professor encouraged, even required, a cognitive journey and effort to build a bridge between our own experiences and those that we are going to offer our future students. As pupils in the class, we were always recalling our experiences as students, thinking about ourselves as growing future teachers, and developing aspirations for our realized classrooms. This professor, Dr. Noulton, (pseudonym), was the first of a series of people in my collegiate experience that–from day one–regarded me as a capable peer. Dr. Noulton, Dr. Salbert, Dr. Tappen, and Dr. Herbert were and are the professional educators that I want to be. At no moment in their classrooms were students' needs or thoughts or confusions trivialized. Each of those individual teachers truly modeled for me (and their students) the respect, preparation, continued learning, shining confidence and care that every pupil needs to become a life long learner; moreover, it is crucial for those traits to be shown to the individuals who will continue the cycle of modeling. The influential professors are doing what they asked us, prospective teachers, to do.

Importance of Community

> At any given time in any given place, there will be a set of conditions—social, historical, meteorological, physiological—that will insure that a word uttered in that place and at that time will have a different meaning than it would have under any other conditions; all utterances are heteroglot in that they are functions of a matrix of forces practically impossible to recoup, and therefore impossible to resolve. (Bakhtin, 1986, p. 428)

> Without dialogue, there is no communication and without communication there can be no true education. (Freire, 1970, p. 81)

Open communication and dialogue occur within a community, so creating a sense of community is vital in terms of establishing an environment in which all students learn. With this end in mind, throughout my years of teaching, I have stressed the three "R's" with my students: rights, responsibility, and respect. Defining these concepts and developing associated understandings via student centered activities results in a sense of community. For example, following are some understandings I would develop with my elementary students and post in the classroom:

•Everyone has the right to learn; No one has the right to interfere with anyone else's learning.
•I am responsible for my learning and for assisting the learning of others.
•Everyone has the right to be respected and to have their things respected.

These understandings formed the foundation of our third grade community in El Paso, Texas when Ramon joined our community; these understandings enabled him to blossom. My collaborators also understand the importance of establishing a community. As Emily Marie prepares for her first year of teaching she anticipates how she will build community:

> One way that community will be developed is to make every student feel a part of my classroom. They will be helping me with different classroom jobs. By giving them responsibility I am hoping that everyone will feel a sense of belonging. I also plan on doing leadership and team building activities from time to time where students can find out more about each other and learn how to better work with one another. I want my students to realize that the environment they are in is one where they can feel safe providing quality input. I will stress the importance of respect. Before I start asking my students to think critically about controversial topics I will provide them scaffolding on how to have these group discussions within the classroom. We will have different discussions, conferences, and writings about topics that are not so controversial, to help us get the hang of how to make comments, share opinions, and follow up to others ideas. For example, on the first day of school we will do an activity where each of us tells a fact about ourselves, that we think is really exciting/neat. Two other students will then reply to each fact. Before we start this activity, we will discuss how to make meaningful comments that will build each other up instead of tearing each other down.

Jamie, who is entering her fifth year of teaching, states:

> I teach character education in the beginning of the school year, which helps create a community within the classroom. I use character education words each week as a theme with different projects for each theme. For instance, we work on citizenship for one week and my class creates a citizenship goal as a classroom to create a community. Also, I use problem solving techniques with them during each week to help build responsible learners within the community. For instance, I might give an example of someone not being honest and then we discuss in groups how the person could have solved the problem.

Alena shares how an assignment she incorporated throughout the school year that promoted discussion and reflection helped foster community in her classes during her first year of teaching:

> Swiftly developed and instituted during the first week of school, the biweekly assignment known as MILK, a "backwards acronym" for "What Everyone Should Know," provided pupils a prime opportunity to decide what was important to them. MILK required students to choose significant artifacts and ideas to share with their peers via discussion and focused writing. Besides encouraging revision of MILK writings, the regular assignment certainly helped foster community within each class. The thing about MILK is the continuing, engrossing class discussion that surrounds students' sharing. We even joke about throwing a ball of yarn across the room as we share to illustrate all the connections that are verbalized between the ideas and artifacts brought for MILK.
>
> In October or November, Dannie, one of my freshman students shared a piece about a teenage boy contemplating suicide from a Chicken Soup for the Soul book. Ironically, one of the very few passages I recall reading from Chicken Soup for the

Teenage Soul book was about a boy committing suicide in his yellow Mustang in the driveway of his home; there is now a campaign where students in middle and high school receive a yellow ribbon card to use if they ever feel like they are in a position of personal last resort; all they have to do it hand the card to someone and they can begin to get help for the individual. The day Dannie (pseudonym) shared was a rather serious day for that class. Students shared grief and confusion over suicide being someone's most desperate choice. I told them about my only experience with suicide: I was in elementary school when one of the sixth grade teachers, Mr. Fraolk, the husband in a young family that just welcomed its first baby a few months before, killed himself one morning as his wife was outside putting the baby in the car-seat. I remembered the way the sixth graders walked around in shock. I remembered that the school brought in grief counselors and pastors, anything so the students would have someone to talk to if they wanted to. Even though I was in third grade and they were in sixth grade, I remembered how much they moved around school aimlessly; it probably took two weeks before their class returned to a regular schedule.

By choosing to add my experience to an already serious conversation, I realized I was instantaneously changing from a student who knew a teacher that chose to end his life to a teacher who was able to get help for someone if they were feeling so alone. I felt like I had the weight of the world on my shoulders. Articulating that I would do anything to help them and that death is not the answer had most of the room in tears. There was a lot going on for me; there was a lot going on for them as individuals.

Dialogic spaces are created within communities that enable students to overcome barriers to developing a critically conscious social justice stance.

Alena shares:

Sometimes, students' own perceptions, comfort levels, and fears (momentarily) impeded thinking and discussion. For instance, several front-loading projects preceded a trip to the Indiana Repertory Theatre to see I Have Before Me a Remarkable Document Given to Me by a Young Lady from Rwanda, a remarkable play which tells the story of Juliette, a survivor the 1994 Rwandan genocide that resulted from a decades old conflict between the Hutus and Tutsis. In addition to studying and creating MILK projects in response to the United Nations Universal Declaration of Human Rights, students answered questions from a racial identity survey (http://www.tolerance.org/teach/web/wfc/pdf/section_2/2_07_writing_racial.pdf) found on the Southern Poverty Law Center's website, Tolerance.org. Word got to me from several students that some of their peers were going to "protest" this "racist" assignment. All I could think was, "People usually protest to get their rights, not to opt out of them!" In the end, no one "protested" or failed to do the assignment; instead, we had a great conversation and waded through uneasiness with the topic. I don't know how many times I heard "It's just not something I think about," that day; the fact that they don't have to think about it says a lot. By the time the class met again, the situation had dissipated so that a reflective conversation ensued; in this calm environment, I did inquire how this could be perceived as an insensitive, even "racist" assignment.

Honesty is what I value most in my relationship with all my students. If there is an issue that troubles my students or me, we bring it to the table; Darfur is a prime example. When viewing a "60 Minutes" segment about the modern-day genocide occurring in Darfur, Sudan, I was compelled to share this information with everyone I knew. I elected to use a half-day during the following week to share this fifteen-minute, eye-opening portion of the show with my pupils; after watching students were asked to reflect in their journals for the remainder of our abbreviated class period. Several weeks later, while the freshmen brainstormed ideas for their "Do-Something Adventure" to parallel Huck's adventure, "Dodgeball for Darfur" was born. The twenty-team, co-ed tournament was realized several months later during "Snowcoming" week; the event raised more than one thousand dollars through five-dollar team entry fees, corporate sponsorships, t-shirt sales, a jewelry raffle, door-to-door collections, and audience ticket sales. Students created advertising posters, produced a "package" for the school's televised morning announcements, and secured sponsorships from local businesses.

Within a community, students are viewed as active agents. Students are empowered when we provide them choice as illustrated in Alena's MILK assignment and their "Do Something Adventure." Further, when we give students voice, guided dialogue within a community can create spaces for students to develop a critically conscious social justice stance. The "tools" we bring into our discussions, such as the racial identity survey or the "60 Minutes" segment, are important for developing new understandings and enacting social justice.

Beginning with a Book

> Multicultural literature, especially the works that move individuals outside of their comfort zones, raise critical consciousness, and challenge the status quo is needed.... Teachers at all levels, need to be equipped to use multicultural literature to critique the past and present and conceive of a hopeful future. (Harris and Willis, 2003, p. 829)

Because many of my understandings of the world began with the characters I met in the books I read in my childhood, I emphasize the importance of literature as I help my preservice teachers develop a critically conscious social justice stance. In particular, I view literature reflecting a diverse perspective as a tool for opening dialogic spaces. Rather than using the term multicultural literature in reference to books in which the main character is a member of a "minority" race, I use the term literature reflecting a diverse perspective to refer to tradebooks, regardless of genre, that have a protagonist that is a member of a group that has been traditionally marginalized due to –ISMS, such as racism, ageism, and sexism.

Fortunately, the world of children's literature is no longer "all white." I am amazed at the inclusivity of voices included in today's children's literature. An excellent example of this is in the book, *Witness* (Hesse, 2001). This book is a series of free verse poems in which each poem expresses the view of a character in a Vermont town in 1924. The town is experiencing conflict at the arrival of the Ku Klux Klan. Included in the voices are twelve year-old Leanora, an African American girl and six-year-old Esther who is Jewish. Books, like *Witness,* tend to invite conversations about issues of power and social justice. Unfortunately, many teachers are reluctant to use them to engage their students in critical conversations (Bishop, 2000) and when they do they encounter resistance (Beach, 1997).

With the goals of overcoming reluctance and resistance to the use of these books, and to help my students develop a critically conscious social justice pedagogy, I emphasize the value of literature reflecting a diverse perspective. An insight I have gained is that often my preservice teachers are reluctant/resistant to incorporate these books into their pedagogy due to their perceptions of childhood. Because of this, I provide them with opportunities to reflect both on their perceptions of childhood and their responses to literature reflecting a diverse perspective in a presentation on censorship. An article that forms the base of my presentation is *Controversial Books and Contemporary Children* (Dresang, 2003). The students read and respond to other articles, such as *Exploring Literature with Gay and Lesbian Characters in the Elementary School* (Schall & Kauffmann, 2003). My intent is for them to critically examine their characterization of children/childhood, how that belief affects their response to children's literature (especially in terms of selecting the literature they will include in their elementary curriculum) and to discover if their current positioning will enable students to meet the IRA/NCTE Standards for the English Language Arts, specifically standards 1, 2, and 10:

- Standard 1: Students read a wide range of print and non-print texts to build an understanding of texts, of themselves, and of the cultures of the United States and the world; to acquire new information; to respond to the needs and demands of society and the workplace; and for personal fulfillment.
- Standard 2: Students read a wide range of literature from many periods in many genres to build an understanding of the many dimensions (e.g. philosophical, ethical, aesthetic) of human experience.
- Standard 10: Students participate as knowledgeable, reflective, creative, and critical members of a variety of literacy communities.

Throughout the presentation, I read books that include controversial topics, such as nontraditional gender roles/characteristics and racial issues to my students and have them respond individually to the following response prompts: Would you incorporate this book in your elementary language arts curriculum? Why or why not? After they respond individually, we discuss their responses. Typically, students perceive children-as-innocent-and-in-need-protection and are not comfortable incorporating these books into their curriculum. Through the presentation, they begin to develop an understanding of children-as-capable-and-seeking-connection. This developing understanding is reflected in their contributions to our discussion and their reflections in their learning logs. For example, following is an excerpt from Emily Marie's learning log for *Exploring Literature with Gay and Lesbian Characters in the Elementary School* (Schall & Kauffmann, 2003), an article that conveys children's need for truth regarding this loaded issue and includes their voices.

After reading the article I realized that students even as young as fourth and fifth grade can handle reading/discussion topics that can been seen as "embarrassing." It is important as the teacher to bring up these topics in a sensitive way. I enjoyed the way that Schall and Kauffmann wanted to hear and see the students initial response- and did not pressure them into feeling one way or another. I believe that allowing students to work things out through discussion is always the best way to go, because it allows them to make their own choices.

Entering her fifth year of teaching, Jamie is still embracing social justice in her classroom, primarily through the use of literature reflecting a diverse perspective and discussions. She shares:

I mostly teach social justice through the use of literature that reflects a diverse perspective, such as non-traditional gender roles and a variety of cultures; which helps students to discuss social justice issues in literature circles. Some pictures books that I use are: *Willie's Not the Hugging Kind*, *William's Doll*, and *Amazing Grace*. This past year I only had two girls in my classroom. We read the book *Willie's Not the Hugging Kind*. The main character, Willie, is embarrassed to hug throughout the story because of a friend. In the end, Willie decides that he is the hugging kind. After reading this book, the boys in my classroom discussed how it's not cool to hug in front of people and they thought it was funny that in the end he was the "hugging kind." We discussed how just because he is boy doesn't mean that he can't hug his family anymore.

Alena also incorporates literature reflecting a diverse perspective into her pedagogy in order to help her students develop a critically conscious social justice pedagogy.

Though I do not declare at the beginning of a piece of literature or text "We are going to learn about…treating people fairly, people's needs, etc.," acknowledgement of universal human needs and desires is most certainly circulating through the atmosphere of my classroom, readying to be lassoed into the current conversation at any moment. One of the bulletin boards in my room, covered in black paper, declares: "Welcome to the Human Experience"; the Language Arts classroom is a natural, needed place to talk about the direct and abstract ties between the content and the learners' own lives. While reading, pondering, and responding to, material in class, the situations surrounding instances of the ISMS is quite often discussed, but the specific "-ism" is generally not used—with the exception of commonly used term "racism" while reading *Huck Finn* or "A Raisin in the Sun." Other luminous literature, such as *House on Mango Street*, most definitely saw us talking about the realities of Esperanza's life and the young married lady who was locked in an apartment down the street by her controlling husband and the worrisome episode of wearing the high heels and having a old man comment troublingly. From *The Odyssey*, the remarkable care and dedication of Odysseus's dog Argus was a poignant, positive example of old age, which my students openly discussed and revered.

The Role of Imagination and the Arts

> Imagination is what, above all, makes empathy possible….That is because, of all our cognitive capacities, imagination is the one that permits us to give credence to alternative realities. It allows us to break with the taken for granted, to set aside familiar distinctions and definitions. (Greene, 1995, p. 3)

In order to "see people big," one must empathize, "One must see from the point of view of the participant in the midst of what is happening…"(Greene, 1995, p. 10). When we use our imagination, we exit the reality of first space and enter second space. In doing so, we become able to address the –ISMS, a determinant of the loaded matrix on thirdspace (Miller & Norris, 2007). Although my collaborators have shared experiences in which their students developed empathy for marginalized characters in literature reflecting a diverse perspective, at times students are unable to accept the unfamiliar and will unconsciously reject a text that reflects a diverse perspective (Soter, 1997). Developing empathy requires readers to "try on" the perspectives of these characters and to consider the possible implications of those perspectives in the reader's life, a goal that is difficult to achieve (Smith & Strickland, 2001).

With this in mind, one of the books in which I engage my seminar students is *From Slave Ship to Freedom Road* (Lester & Brown, 1998). In the introduction to this powerful picture book for older readers, Lester states, "Art and literature ask us to step out of our skins and put on the skins of others" (p. 5). The book consists of Brown's somewhat raw paintings depicting slave life, accompanied by text created by Lester. Throughout the text, Lester addresses the reader, pleading readers to imagine themselves in the images and includes numerous imagination exercises. This potent picture-book for older readers can be shared in part with younger readers to engage them in "critical" conversations about the issues of power and social justice. For example, Lester includes the following imagination exercise:

> It is a sunny day. Suddenly a spaceship lands and people of a skin color you have never seen come out of the ship and drag you aboard—you, your family, neighbors, and friends. The ship takes off and flies for three months. When it lands, you are in a place you never knew existed and the people speak a language you have never heard. They have weapons that hurt, maim, and kill. They give you a name—Mammy, Remus, Jemima, Sambo. They do not care what your real name is or who you really are. You are their slave and you exist now to work for them. Imagine a rage so fierce it would scorch the earth, leaving behind only a giant cinder to circle the sun. You do not have to be black to be this angry. Your ancestors need not have been Africans. You need only wonder: How would I feel if that happened to me? When we can imagine the hurt and anger of another, we have an understanding in the heart. When we understand in the heart, each of us is less alone.

As I read this imagination exercise to my seminar students, I show them the painting that accompanies it. The painting depicts a group of African Americans, thoroughly shackled with heavy chains attached to iron collars around their necks, wrists and ankles, standing together with grim expressions on their faces wearing only white loincloths. I have my seminar students respond in either a quickwrite or a quickdraw (a method for responding to literature that enables students to reflect and develop ideas about a topic). We discuss their responses and reflect on the process. How and why did they develop empathy? The painting provides us with access to the imagined experience of the "other," enabling us to develop empathy. As Dewey (1934) asserts, art "strikes below the barriers that separate human beings from each other…. Art renders men [and women] aware of their union with one another in origin and destiny" (p. 272).

My seminar students and I begin to explore further the power of images in children's literature reflecting a diverse perspective in terms of helping classroom students develop a critically conscious social justice stance. Photo essays, in which the text and photos work together to convey meaning, are especially powerful. *Through My Eyes* (Bridges, 1999) is an excellent example. In this photo essay, Ruby Bridges tells the story of her experiences as the only black child in an all-white school when the federal government enforced integration in the public schools in New Orleans in 1960. A terrifying image is a photograph of demonstrators outside of the school. Ruby had to pass them on her way into the school. The demonstrators, mostly women and children, are smiling at the camera; several of them are holding signs opposing integration or other objects. For example, one young boy is holding a black doll in a coffin. With this image in front of us, we empathize. *Imagine walking past this crowd on your way to school as a first-grade student. How do you feel? How do you keep walking?*

Jamey shares an experience she had with her second graders that illustrates the power of images in picture books reflecting a diverse perspective to open spaces for critical dialogue:

> We were doing a civil rights movement unit in class. We were reading a book, *If you Lived at the Time of Martin Luther King*. This is an informational picture book with questions and answers. The students came to a page that had pictures of slaves and people from the KKK. My class had many questions about why the white people had on these costumes. I had to explain to my second graders that there are people that are racist and they wore these costumes to show that they are part of a group called the KKK. We had to have a discussion about the pictures and it was hard to explain everything to my class. Many of the students wanted to know why the white people were so horrible to the black people. I brought in other picture books to read together and websites to research more about the civil rights movement. Being able to look at photographs from the time period is helpful.

Later on in the semester my seminar students and I discuss the power of transmediation, an insight I have gained through my research. Transmediation occurs when meanings initiated in one communication system are moved to an alternate communication system (e.g. from reading to writing to oral to visual). This process provides students with opportunities to reflect consciously on concepts and elaborate on them, forming new connections between existing concepts (Rice, 2002). Of particular importance is engagement with several arts. As Greene (1995) notes, "informed engagements with the several arts is the most likely mode of releasing our students' (or any persons') imaginative capacity and giving it play"(p. 125).

It is in this discussion that we move beyond the power of illustrations and focus on dramatization, dramatizing at the center of the text and moving to dramatization at the edges of the text. When dramatizing at the center of the text, readers assume the role of the characters and remain true to the dialogue and plot written on the page (Wolf, Edmiston, & Enciso, 1997). This activity is known as *reader's theater* in which the text is changed into a script with a narrator and actors engaging in the dialogue as it appears in the text. Dramatizing at the edges of the text, is sometimes referred to as educational drama (Bolton, 1979; Heathcote, 1984). When dramatizing at the edges of the text, students enter the story world and engage in imaginary interactions that are implied by the circumstances of the story. When working with students of all ages, I have discovered it is easier for them to move to the edges of the text after they have engaged in dramatization at the center of the text.

For example, I have created a readers' theater script of the picture storybook *The Story of Ruby Bridges* (Coles, 1995). The readers' theater script includes the following voices: narrator, Ruby, Ruby's mother, and Miss Hurley (Ruby's first grade teacher). The illustrations depict other characters in the story world that do not speak directly in the text, such as Ruby's brother and sister, Ruby's father, the federal marshals and the angry white mob outside of the Frantz Elementary School. The illustrations enable us to enter the story world and begin to imagine other conversations. So, after engaging in readers' theater I have my students move to the edges of the text by engaging in drama conversations (Wolf & Enciso, 1994)—small groups engaged in improvisation among, for example, (a) Ruby's parents, (b) the angry white mob outside of Frantz Elementary School, (c) the federal marshals, (d) teachers at the Frantz Elementary School, (d) parents of white children who formerly attended Frantz Elementary School, (e) white children who formerly attended Frantz Elementary School. I also have some students play the role of newspaper reporters sent onto the scene by me, their editor. After the dramatizations, we debrief and reflect on the process, my students unanimously agree that the drama conversations are difficult when portraying someone who has a perspective different from their own, but effective in terms of "seeing big."

Beginnings…

> Coming to voice is not just the act of telling one's experience. It is using that telling strategically—to come to voice so that you can also speak freely about other subjects. (hooks, 1994, p. 148)

> All we can do is to speak with others as passionately and eloquently as we can; all we can do is to look into each other's eyes and urge each other on to new beginnings. Our classrooms ought to pulsate with multiple conceptions of what it is to be human and alive. They ought to resound with the voices of articulate young people in dialogues always incomplete because there is always more to be discovered and more to be said. We must want our students to achieve friendship as each one stirs to wide-awakeness, to imaginative action, and to renewed consciousness of possibility. (Greene, 1995, p. 43)

Usually, one perceives the end of a chapter as a conclusion, an ending, but as I pull things together, I envision beginnings. In the introduction sj asks, "Collectively, can we move towards a space that we have yet to materialize such that teachers can practice and embody pedagogies that are unequivocally authentic? And what would those spaces look like which would enable teachers to materialize those pedagogies and subjectivities?" As I stated at the beginning of this chapter, writing this narrative has been an insightful journey for me in which I engaged in what sj calls the 5 "re-s" of "fourthspace": reflect, reconsider, reconceptualize, rejuvenate and reengage." An important insight I gained is the value of the 5 "re-s" in terms of uniting mind and body so that one is able to embody a critical pedagogy. So in answer to sj's questions…*Yes. We can move toward a space that will enable teachers to practice and embody authentic pedagogies—fourthspace.*

As Dewey (1938/1963) emphasizes, continuity between past and present experience leads to human growth:

> Different situations succeed one another. But because of the principle of continuity something is carried over from the earlier to the later ones. As an individual passes from one situation to another, his [sic] world, his environment, expands or contracts. He does not find himself living in another world but in a different part or aspect of one and the same world. What he has learned in the way of knowledge and skill in one situation becomes an instrument of understanding and dealing effectively with the situations which follow. (p. 42)

Reflection is a vital skill. As sj notes in the introduction, "Reflection can lead to change and by engaging teachers in such opportunities we can help them on their way to social justice teaching; even when they may be far away from the safety of our classrooms" (p. 11). Unfortunately, for me, I did not know the value of reflection in terms of understanding my identity positionings as configured by societal markers of race, class and gender until I was a doctoral student. So, although I embodied a strong sense of social justice when I taught elementary school, I was naïve about the impact of differing sociopolitical agendas. Due to my experiences, I was able to "see things and people big," but I lacked voice and was unable to navigate the intransigent educational system. Because of this, in Ramon's case, I was unable to enact social justice in my teaching.

When I met Alena this past summer at the *WILLA* summer meeting, her strong voice compelled me to invite her to collaborate. When I asked her, "How has reflection been a part of your identity as a social justice educator? How has reflection enabled you to reconceptualize your thinking in ways that are more aligned with your belief system?" she responded:

> It feels like I have always carried seeds of this caring and enthusiasm, but I had not been as vocal and active until I realized I was an important part of other people's lives, even a role model as some might call it. And I would much rather be a role model with a gigantic heart who cares and desires to do something than a mint condition Barbie doll, or teacher, in a box; at the end of my career, I don't want to be a teacher who has never had ups and downs, or ached with concern for the kids and content; I don't want to simply punch my time card, recite my lesson plans, put up my overhead slides, and count the minutes until the bell rings like a disinterested pupil. So, teaching with a social action foundation is a recursive system where I feel responsible to my students. It is a situation where they fortify my confidence and seemingly eliminate the possibility of individual self-doubt, because the collective is stronger. There's something that exists in a living, breathing classroom; these students are not an adult audience: they are not jaded; they are not professional skeptics. Mind you, these fourteen, fifteen, sixteen year olds that I work for and with, show the most genuine concern and compassion for injustices and issues existing in the world; sometimes, I think they are happy to see somebody who has as much enthusiasm as they do.
>
> Reflection has enabled me to re-conceptualize my actions in ways that are more in line with my belief system. I care about things–people, the environment, peace, and the future—so I am going to try! I feel like I know it's ok to care; I couldn't be happier with a profession where that is my job. My students and I get to effort toward something meaningful. We're putting our thought, time, creativity, care into responding to disconcerting aspects of our world; we're taking advantage of opportunities to be constructive in the world. Specifically related to the Social Action endeavors during my first year of teaching, reflection, hope, and the impossibility of being shamed for my, our attempts, made it a prime time to ask myself and my pupils, "Why not?" "Why not sponsor a child in a third-world country?" And, they decided to do that. "Let's have a dodgeball tournament." I offered the possibility for Social Action and they ran with it. Though students suggested a myriad of means to make a difference, the fact that I had the self-possession to help them achieve their elected goals is amazing; I cannot wait to return to this collaborative, productive groove. Coupled with the positive experiences of taking my ninth and tenth Honors classes on multiple field trips to the local repertory theatre, the unique pursuits of sponsoring Sai from Sri Lanka and sponsoring a school-wide dodgeball tournament and awareness campaign against the genocide in Darfur, Sudan, have saved me from ever feeling like a first year failure or like some-

body who lets the kids down; I know no matter what, they will have things to remember distinctly and proudly.

Unfortunately, not all first year-teachers are able to enact a social justice pedagogy like Alena. For many, the realities of federal, state, and local mandates provide constraints and quite often, as sj notes in the introduction, beginning teachers return to what is familiar to them—a traditional paradigm of teaching, a fact I discovered when I was seeking collaborators. Consequently an important insight for me has been to provide continuity as my students transition from preservice to inservice spaces that will enable the dialogic spaces we developed to continue. With this in mind, I created an external community in blackboard—"fourthspace." The purpose of this community is to provide beginning teachers, who had elementary English language arts as their concentration area (my former ENG 401 students), a space to communicate (reflect, reconceptualize, rejuvenate and reengage) as they navigate the politics of teaching elementary English language arts, so that they are better able to align their teaching practices with their beliefs.

As my spring 2007 seminar students, enter their first year of teaching, they envision using imagination and the arts with literature reflecting a diverse perspective in order to help their students develop a critically conscious social justice stance. Emily Marie reflects back on her student teaching, reconsiders her selection of literature, and reconceptualizes her pedagogy:

> As I go into my first year of teaching I hope to present issues that go along with these social justices more than I have in the past. While reading "Sign of the Beaver" in literature circles during student teaching we discussed the fairness of forcing Native Americans out of their homeland. I brought up subjects of white settlers having the mindset that they were better than the Native Americans. It is not often that we hear the side of the Native Americans. Looking back now, I could kick myself for not finding text that demonstrates these other viewpoints. As I was thinking that I was promoting social justice by talking about these issues, I did nothing to further the thinking. I have recently been looking for books from the Native American's views, which I will keep next to "The Sign of the Beaver" in my collection. While looking back on student teaching I see that there are many other times in which I could have used more literature to illustrate different points that the students discussed in class. While the discussion is an important aspect, I should have been adding literature also. During my first year of teaching I am going to have a basically all-White classroom, which does not show other sides or perspectives as much as I would like. Focusing again on the "Sign of the Beaver" unit I did while student teaching, I am aware now that I will need to find these other perspectives to present to my classroom. This summer I have tried to find texts that show what it was like for different minorities to go through the historical events that my students will usually only see one side of. For example I have bought books that show opposing viewpoints of the Holocaust, immigration to America, growing up in slavery, being forced to move because of white settlers, growing up without a family, and children who have abusive/ non-existent parents. I feel that by showing my students alternate viewpoints they will be able to create their own opinions

and views on subjects, rather that just continuing on with what they have been told by others in the past. I will also provide opportunities for my students to "feel/re-live" what life was like for others, as well as just reading about it. I would like for my students to engage in activities that will help them visualize what life was like for the characters. This could be through drama or interviews with people.

The school that I will be teaching at this up-coming year has a student body that will not have had much experience with different races. This is information I have received both from my Principal and the Indiana State Elementary School Statistics. The student body at the school is over 99% white. My Principal has also let me know that racial issues and socio-economical issues are subjects that have not typically been discussed by any teacher in the school with students, in the past. I feel that in the past the feelings towards these topics have been that since my students are not affected by this on a day-to-day basis it does not need to be brought to the surface. I disagree.

Will institutional practices create barriers for Emily Marie? Most likely. Will "fourthspace" enable her to overcome those barriers? Most likely. Greene (1988) urges us to "discover how to open spaces for persons in their plurality, spaces where they can become different, where they can grow (p. 56)." I believe "fourthspace" is that space.

References

Bakhtin, M. M. (1986). *Speech genres and other late essays.* Austin: University of Texas Press.

Beach, R. (1997). Students' resistance to engagement in responding to multicultural literature. In T. Rogers & A. O. Soter (Eds.), *Reading across cultures: Teaching literature in a diverse society* (pp. 69-94). New York: Teachers College Press.

Bishop, R. (2000, December). *Cross-disciplinary Perspectives on children's and young adult literature.* Paper presented at the National Reading Conference, Scottsdale, Arizona.

Bolton, G. (1979). *Towards a theory of drama in education.* London: Longman.

Bridges, R. (1999). *Through my eyes.* New York: Scholastic.

Coles, R. (1995). *The story of Ruby Bridges.* New York: Scholastic.

Commeyras, M. (2002). Provocative questions that animate my thinking about teaching. *Language Arts, 80 (2),* 129-133.

Dewey, J. (1938/1963). *Experience and education.* New York: Macmillan.

Dewey, J. (1934). *Art as experience.* New York: Perigee.

Dodge, M. M. (1865). *Hans Brinker or the silver skates.* London: Sampson Low, Marston Low & Searle.

Dresang, E. T. (2003) Controversial books and contemporary children. *Journal of Children's Literature,* 29(1), 20-31.

Freire, P. (1970). *Pedagogy of the oppressed.* New York: Continuum Publishing.

Greene, M. (1988). *The dialectic of freedom.* New York: Teachers College Press.

Greene, M. (1995). *Releasing the imagination.* San Francisco: Jossey-Bass.

Harris, V.J. & Willis, A.I. (2003). Multiculturalism, literature, and curriculum issues. In J. Flood, D. Lapp, J. Squire & J. Jensen (Eds.), *Handbook of research on teaching the English language arts.* (pp. 825-833). Mahwah: Lawrence Erlbaum.

Heathcote, D. (1984). Drama as challenge. In L. Johnson & C. O'Neill (Eds.), *Dorothy Heathcote: Collected writing on education and drama* (pp. 80-89). Evanston: Northwestern University Press.

Heilbrun, C. (1988). *Writing a woman's life.* New York: Norton.

Hesse, K. (2001). *Witness.* New York: Scholastic Press.

hooks, b. (1994). *Teaching to transgress: Education as the practice of freedom.* New York: Routledge.

Larrick, N. (1965). The all white world of children's books. *Saturday Review* (September 11), 63-65, 84-85.

Lester, J. & Brown, R. (1998). *From slave ship to freedom road.* New York: Scholastic.

Miller, s., & Norris, L. (2007). *Unpacking the loaded teacher matrix: Negotiating space and time between university and secondary English classrooms.* New York: Peter Lang.

Rice, P. (2002). Creating spaces for boys and girls to expand their definitions of masculinity and femininity through children's literature, *Journal of Children's Literature, 28* (2), 33-40.

Schall, J. & Kauffmann, G. (2003). Exploring literature with gay and lesbian characters in the elementary school. *Journal of Children's Literature,* 29(1), 36-45.

Smith, M.W. & Strickland, D.S. (2001). Complements or conflicts: Conceptions of discussion and multicultural literature in a teachers-as-readers discussion group. *Journal of Literacy Research, 33* (1), 137-167.

Soja, E. W. (1996). *Thirdspace: Journeys to Los Angeles and other real-and-imagined places.* Malden: Blackwell.

Soter, A.O. (1997). Reading literature of other cultures. In T. Rogers & A.O. Soter (Eds.), *Reading across cultures: Teaching Literature in a Diverse Society* (pp. 213-229). New York: Teachers College Press.

Steinbeck, J. (1992). *The grapes of wrath.* New York: Penguin.

White, E. B. (1952). *Charlotte's web.* New York: Scholastic.

Wolf, S., Edmiston, B., & Enciso, P. (1997). Drama worlds: Places of the heart, head, voice, and hand in dramatic interpretation. In J. Floord, S.B. Heath & D. Lapp (Eds.), *Handbook of research on teaching literacy through the communicative and visual arts* (pp. 492-505). New York: Macmillan.

Wolf, S. & Enciso, P. (1994). Multiple selves in literary interpretation: Engagement and the language of drama. In C.K. Kinzer & D. J. Leu (Eds.), *Multidimensional aspects of literacy research, theory, and practice* (Forty-third Yearbook of National Reading Conference)(pp. 351-360). Chicago: National Reading Conference.

5

Multicultural Spaces Meet Rural Places

sj Miller with Channell Wilson-Segura and Kristy Lorenzo

The collaboration for this chapter is very exciting for the three of us. We decided to each write separately and then braid our stories together later. Currently, we each teach in very different spaces: sj, in a rural university in Western, PA with a fairly ethnically homogenous (white) population though with small pockets of diversity; Channell, in a multicultural city in the Southwest in a fairly diverse high school; and Kristy, in a rural/suburban, fairly ethnically homogenous (white) middle school in Western, PA. Our lives have entwined collectively for the past eight years and though sj knows both Channell and Kristy, they have never met face-to-face. Eight years ago, while in the Southwest, Channell was sj's student during her secondary English teaching licensure program in a course entitled "Creating a Critically Conscious Teaching Pedagogy" and later became sj's student teacher in a multicultural high school. Two years ago, Kristy was in a course taught by sj entitled "Teaching Reading in the Secondary Schools" and was supervised by sj last year during her preservice teaching placement during her secondary English teacher preparation program in Western, PA. Collectively, our narrative explores how we each came to terms with our social justice pedagogies and identities, and details how we each have applied and experienced necessary tensions when we have unpacked and taught social justice in our classrooms and our lives beyond.

sj

Growing up in Metairie, Louisiana in a middle-class, Jewish family that held overtly prejudicial beliefs, I somehow managed to come out with a heightened consciousness that what my parents said about people of color was morally wrong. I have often wondered how I came to know this from an early age and perhaps it was my due to my positive encounters during early schooling days where I did not understand differences based on color, class, gender, or ability. Prejudice was taught at home yet school leveled any playing field that my parents had tried to un-level. Although we spoke English at home, that language was peppered with cussing and yelling; though, my parents were painfully literate in spite of their propensity to utilize four letter words. Profanity was a way of life, as was drinking, cheating, eating disorders, extortion, police, divorce(s), physical, sexual and emotional abuse, suicide, but above all was a reverence for education, which became my higher power.

My first true awakening about understanding the concept of prejudice began when I'd asked permission to bring a friend home from kindergarten after school. With permission secured, my boyfriend Tyrone and I took the school bus home as happy as two kindergartners in love could be. We innocently exited the bus and approached the front door. My mom opened the front door, looked at me and then looked at Tyrone, did a double-take of Tyrone, yanked me inside the door and silently screamed at me, "You will never bring a black child to this home again, ya' hear?"-(although Black was a euphemism for what she actually said). In all honesty, I had no idea what she meant. I was five and innocent, and Tyrone was my friend and this experience was my ugly introduction to issues based on skin color. After this incident, I became acutely aware of how others around me were treated because of their skin color and my heightened awareness of what had transpired as a five year old would remain a turning point for me for the rest of my life.

Both of my parents were college educated. My mom was an English and math teacher and my father was an infectious disease doctor. My parents enrolled me in private school to "protect" me from the evils of difference. School entailed reading, catered lunches, field trips, playing with metrics, puzzles and being constantly engaged in problem-solving activities. Not only was I enrolled in private school but I also attended Hebrew school and learned my Hebrew alphabet and how to read and write the language. Hebrew school became more of a competition about who had the latest and most fashionable styles and toys and ceased to be a positive experience for me. Private school did anything but "protect" me as it made me aware of how privileged I was and how much I detested it.

When I turned eight my life literally fell apart. Suddenly, it was made clear that daddy was "shtooping" the nurse at work and mommy was leaving him. My younger sister and I were caught in the midst of a turbulent tug-of-war, resulting in a kidnapping to Florida. I was ripped from my father and planted somewhere in the inferno of Dade County. With enough screaming and yelling, my mom let me return to Metairie, Louisiana and live with my father while she found a new spouse and raised my little sister, Jill. My father remarried and I gained a step-mom and two step-brothers. We moved to southern California where I enrolled in public school for the first time in my life in the fourth grade. I struggled with the public school system and felt it was much harder than the schools from where I'd just come. In so many aspects, it seemed that I was ill prepared for public school. The private school had sheltered me from lower class kids and nurtured me to think I was more capable and smarter than I was.

Floundering in public school, I realized I was finally challenged academically for the first time in my life and that I would have to work hard if I were to do well. At the same time as this lifestyle change, my stepbrother began sexually abusing me and I escaped into a fantasy world of endless reading, athletics and studying. I was drawn to VC Andrews series, *Flowers in the Attic* which became my only solace. My father and stepmother were heavy drinkers and would fight, hit, and then make up. I lived in their constant crossfire. There was neither love nor communication in that home and I knew then that I needed to leave: silence became my means of communication—and I was only nine.

Three years down the road, I moved to join my mom, stepfather and sister who relocated to Santa Fe, New Mexico. Once again, I changed schools, friends and home environments. This time though, back with my mom, a heavy emphasis was placed on learning and attending Hebrew school again. I took to the challenge and started earning straight A's and excelling in soccer and swimming. Soccer and swimming served to channel my feelings around the emotional and sexual abuse. They became ways to save me, to guide me, to make me work through the pain and loss; they became my aspects of my higher power and a huge part of my self-esteem.

Year after year in public school I earned straight A's and racked up honors playing soccer. Home seemed almost "normal," although visitation to my father's home continued and so did my sexual and physical abuse. During eighth grade, a landmark event happened though which changed the course of my ability to read and feel confident about my schooling. I had earned straight A's all the way through junior high and was taking an honor's reading course, when two-thirds through the year, the students in eighth grade had to take a standardized test in reading. Not only did I fail that exam miserably, but I was removed from the honor's class and my friends and placed in remedial reading. Fortunately, the teacher, whose class into which I moved, knew that I didn't belong in her room and allowed me to become her teacher's aid. However, I spent the rest of that year thinking that I could not read or write well. That event has tragically scarred me and I still freeze up whenever I think about standardized tests and "right" answers.

High school was a breeze academically, but personally it was beyond tragic. Soccer honors racked up, the 4.0 grew, honor society, student council, friends, boyfriends, popularity, I had it all. But then my stepdad ran out on my family in the middle of the night during my sophomore year and we never heard from him again. My mom succumbed to an insensible depression. One year later, my grandmother committed suicide, left me the suicide note, and my mom checked out of life after that. My sister and I parented ourselves through the rest of high school and worked to support a mom who was barely able to function. We fell from middle class, right into poverty. We moved from apartment to apartment because the rent was always too high. I lived on the couch my senior year of high school because we could not afford a three bedroom home. Fortunately, because I had somehow maintained my 4.0 throughout high school and graduated salutatorian, and because I was so strong academically, I had top division one schools recruiting me to play soccer in college. Without hesitation, I prematurely left home for college and entered U.C. Berkeley for the next four years. The one thing I applaud my mother for was her strict, totalitarian law: "If you don't get straight A's, you don't come home" and that inspired me to work diligently in high school; it was her way of saying, I can't be there for you so you need to do it for yourself.

The next four years of my life at Berkeley, I worked more diligently than I had ever worked. I studied, played soccer, traveled with the US Women's National Team, found my niche with other feminist Jews, started teaching Hebrew school, "came out of the closet," and was disowned by my father for my queer identity. My mother stopped speaking to me, and my stepmother left my father. I grew extremely depressed and isolated. The one strand of constancy that kept motivating me from killing myself was education, reading, and athletics. Somehow, in the deep of the night and through the words of authors and theoreticians, I found my escape and it silenced the negative voice in my head that said I wasn't good enough. At Cal, I was exposed to amazing diverse professors like Cherrie Moraga, Thomas Almaguer, Trinh Minh-ha, June Jordan, Nancy Chodorow, Arlie Hochschild, MaryAnn Mason, and from that point forward, I could never read or learn enough. That brooding exposed me to a new world or poetry and queer gender theory and awakened an untapped sense of my needs around understanding differences based on race, class, gender, sexual orientation, ability, age, religion, appearance and finally gave voice to my extended silence—I was nineteen. I devoured books. My Jewish feminism grew, and my new culture formed around my new Jewish, queer identity. I became radical and fierce and decided that it was "Ok" to be who I was even if my family no longer wanted to be part of my life. I knew that I had to work hard on my studies and that would empower me to help myself...and it did. I graduated with high honors, left Cal to do my master's in Jewish Studies at the Hebrew Union College and toyed with the notion of going into the rabbinate. When I finished my master's, I moved back to Santa Fe and teaching found me.

I have spent the last fourteen years teaching a variety of levels in public school and am now a secondary English education professor. At the heart of my teaching is exposing my teachers to different pedagogies and helping support them in their brooding development to embody a social justice agenda. Before the academic year always begins, I always consider which voices need to be heard in my classroom, what social and political issues are current, and how I can be open to new works and authors. When teaching, I am careful to consider a balanced curriculum, which means exposing my students to both side of any issue while also crafting opportunities for them to explore how power, privilege and oppression manifest in school spaces and even in their own identities. My students see me model different approaches to teaching that align with my own social justice agenda—which I make clear from the beginning of our course-work. I invite critique and by no means require them to adopt my pedagogy. My hope is that they will embody a pedagogy that aligns with their belief systems. This is critical because instructors may inadvertently silence students. We

> Must allow ideas to emerge without imposing their own bias. In this way, students are more likely to talk and the instructor can then negotiate the flow of dialogue by posing open-ended questions. Although the instructor may disagree with a student's position-ality that may seem prejudiced, we dishonor our work to social justice when we silence students who may have a view that is dissonant from others or even our own. We must work at developing our skills to negotiate the flow of dialogue and be willing to let stu-dents teach us about themselves even when we may perceive it as loaded. (Miller & Norris, 2007, p.161)

I know I can't change from where I came, and how others have been treated, but I can change where I am going and how I act in the world. In many ways I did come from privilege because I always had shelter and at least one parent and am grateful for what I was given and though my life has been diffi-cult and am in limited contact with my family still, I am content; I have found how to bring pleasure into my life and how to take care of myself even when others won't or can't. Privilege manifests itself differently for each person and even how each person understands what privilege means. I wouldn't be who I am today had I not gone through what I did. I allow my own life experiences to guide me on a quest for justice for all people. I have thought long and hard how my parents behaved in the world toward others and myself and that has moti-vated me to want to understand and probe deeper into the human psyche. It is my intention to bring the world a person/teacher who embodies empathy and love, and gift students with the desire to learn, to have agency, to empower them with self-knowledge and encourage them live up their potential. This means I live by example. I volunteer when I am needed, I stand up for others in the face of adversity, I am an ally, I vote, I challenge the binary, I represent, and I do not take lightly to setbacks but use them to learn from and move on. As Gandhi said, "Be the change you wish to see in the world," and that is exactly how I aspire to live and teach.

Channell

Ever since I was a young girl in my own journey through elementary educa-tion I knew that I wanted to be a teacher. My stepfather had a chalkboard in his office that I would use during my summer vacations to write vocabulary words and arithmetic problems on for my students. Of course my students at that time were a well-behaved semicircle of empty water buckets. It was a wonderful experience and it all came so naturally to me. I remember buying my first pack of chalk and the excitement of returning to my chalkboard. I would draw lines across the board so that my work was even and neat. I even had a whistle to mimic the bell system that designated the segments of time for each subject. As I recall that vivid memory, I wonder what it was that early in my childhood influenced me to pursue a career as an educator, especially a secondary educator. I was young and naïve to the reality that teaching was not as simple as teaching students who would sit quietly, wouldn't question my authority, who would complete their assignments on time, and who were not critical to the racial, social, sexual, economic, and other differences in each other or in me. I did this not realizing the complexities I would encounter as I later ventured to become what I practiced so vigorously as a young girl in my stepfather's office, a public school teacher.

My full name is Channell Monique Wilson-Segura. Wilson is my maiden name as well as the surname of my Anglo stepfather who adopted me when I was fifteen years old. Segura is my married name. I hyphenated my surname when I married because when my stepfather adopted me I realized that there is more meaning to it than just a name. My skin is what one would consider brown, and growing up in a predominately Hispanic community, my last name was always questioned; I was always questioned. It was frustrating because at the time I did not know the reasons for that. Later on in my life, I would learn that the last name Wilson was not a "Hispanic" surname. My identity was being shaped by what others thought of me as a child, and as I grew up, I found myself explaining who and what I was to many ignorant individuals.

When I graduated from high school in the spring of 1998, I attended the University of New Mexico where I received a bachelor of arts in English and dance, and recently completed a master of arts there in secondary education. I am a native of Santa Fe, New Mexico which is also the city where I currently teach. In fact, the high school where I teach is my alma mater. The city itself has transformed over the past ten years due to the growing Mexican immigrant population. When I was in high school, the majority of the population consisted of the local Hispanics/Chicanos, followed by an Anglo population, and an almost non-existent African American population. In high school, my friend Cole was the only black male in our school at the time and we even teased him because he spoke like a Chicano; it was all in good fun. He was a mutual friend of my husband's and mine, and we named our son after him. At that time, there was a small minority of Mexican immigrant students; in fact, I cannot even recall more than a handful of them.

Ten years later, I feel like a minority because of the continual rise of Mexican immigrants entering my community at a very rapid rate. I have overheard and conversed with many people who have expressed their feelings about the overwhelming influence and growth of the Mexican population. They all seem to have the same stance on the subject; they explain that these individuals need to learn English if they want the respect and recognition that they expect. I too felt that way at one point, but have now come to the realization that in order to co-exist with this population, I need to take the initiative to learn Spanish in order to be respected and to respect these individuals. One might ask why I need to speak their language in order to be respected. It is not that I do not have the respect of my Mexican students and their families, because I know that I am able to accomplish this early in the academic school year through much patience, compassion, empathy, and effort. The respect I am looking for is the cultural understanding and connection that comes from within my own being and emanates my students.

In my classroom and in the hallways during passing periods, students speak to one another in Spanish. I practice my Spanish speaking skills by listening to them and responding to them with my limited Spanish vocabulary. However, my colleagues and I are faced with the challenge of teaching these students the vital skills they need to compete with other students, schools, and districts. As an English teacher, I expect every student of mine to communicate with one another and me in English. This is not because I do not appreciate their native language; in fact, I wish I were fluent in it. I am in a situation where students come to me with limited English vocabulary and syntax, and I am expected to teach them to the point where they can be functional members of this society. I put my heart and soul into creating an environment for my students where they will feel safe against the ridicule, demeaning torments, and embarrassment they face by their peers, and even some of their teachers with embedded racial conflicts, when they make mistakes in their writing and verbalizations. Unfortunately, racism is entrenched within this community and my academic institution, and it directly affects the learning process needed for the healthy socialization and sustainability of the diverse cultures and individuals within it.

I have always had an appreciation for all people no matter how different they were from me. I would be lying if I said that I have never prejudged individuals or groups of individuals based on their inherent genetic compositions, beliefs, or preferences. It is through my own educational journey and through respectful interaction with people who do not share my same beliefs or preferences, that I have grown to be the person that I can respect due to my growing appreciation for all beings no matter who or what they are. I am conscious of the labels that have been placed upon groups of people; however, through my exposure to people of different races, cultures, and beliefs while in college and through my professional experiences, I can say I am more aware of the repercussions of ignorance and hate.

One individual, who created an awareness of the importance of social justice, and how to emulate it from within my own pedagogy, was the supervisor and cooperative teacher I was placed with throughout my pre-service teaching: Dr. Miller. As I observed her, I began to take notice of her extreme passion for teaching students the importance of human understanding and compassion. It was through this exposure that I observed her students become more considerate and respectful of the differences in her and one another. It did not matter what novel she taught, she always made her students aware of the social effect each text had on society. She did not just teach the standard raw material that many English teachers get away with; she took risks by cultivating discussions with her students about the importance of the author's background, the targeted audience, the political stances, and the effect of the time period in which it was published. At times the classroom environment became very critical, emotional, and unstable, but a pre-established standard of respect was always existent. Her passion for accepting everyone was what shaped me as a first-year teacher to teach beyond the pages.

Kristy

I grew up in a small town in Northwestern Pennsylvania. My graduating class had eighty-nine students, and we knew everyone's families and "business." My mother is a teacher and my father is self-employed in the logging business. Both of my parents are extremely hard workers, and I always used that fact to justify me driving a new car or wearing expensive clothes. In school I could easily fit in with most social groups though in thinking back now on how my fellow classmates treated each other is a difficult thing to do. Often, I stood with the crowd who made fun of the "scudders," the lower class students. I was guilty only by association. I never opened my mouth to taunt anyone, but I admit I laughed at times. I always felt horrible inside as I watched classmates being humiliated just for being themselves. At the time I didn't see the bullying as an issue of power, but as an adult and teacher, I know that bullying and oppressing others is rooted in gaining power and finding self-assurance.

Now looking back, I see why I chose to be a teacher for several reasons. At first, I wanted to be an English teacher so I could teach people ways to express themselves through writing and dialogue. I also wanted to share my passion for reading, and I hoped to help people connect to books, poetry, and other genres. I just knew that I would return to the classroom and teach the assigned readings with a breath of fresh air. By my second semester of college I already learned that I could accomplish much more as an English teacher. My second semester included a class called Literary Analysis. Literary Analysis did so much more than just teach me to analyze literature; it opened my eyes to the "ISMS" and social inequalities. It was the first time I had the official tools to analyze and to question the actions and words of the people around me as well as my own.

Along with opening my eyes to the world of oppression, the class helped me to find my voice and use it in class and in my writing. I was asked to include my opinion in all response papers. I had never been "allowed" to write using "I," and I could not believe a professor cared about my personal opinion. Immediately, I knew I wanted my future students to take their masks off and write with their voices. At first, addressing and discussing issues like classism, sexism, and racism was very difficult for me. I was often silenced because I felt that I was somehow going to offend someone by talking openly. I watched my professor use teaching strategies to help students feel part of a community and with that community there came trust. I kept thinking where would I be if I never entered this class? Would I have continued the rest of my life in the small town bubble thinking that social injustices were a city problem? I will probably always teach in rural school districts, so it is important for me to bring aspects of social justice into the classroom. I want to diminish the small town mentality. I was frustrated; I wanted to help students find their voice and recognize social injustices and do something to conquer it.

The next semester after taking Literary Analysis, I interviewed my high school superintendent because I was writing a paper that critiqued Pennsylvania's Standardized Tests (PSSA). After I asked all of my planned questions, she asked me what I was most looking forward once I was a certified teacher. At that point in my college career, I wasn't sure I even wanted to teach. I felt so confined by the Department of Education's standards, and I had lost hope because I felt I would never have the freedom to address important issues in my future classroom. Regardless of my conflicting thoughts, I told the superintendent I wanted to help students read the world with a critical eye and express their thoughts in writing. I told her that I knew I couldn't really teach theory and address the big issues in public schools. She simply said, "Write a sound rationale statement, and I think a good administrator would let you tackle the issues. What you are saying is important." I saw a glimmer of hope, and I settled back into believing I wanted to teach.

My teacher education courses continued and I filed information for later reference; however, I remember very clearly the day I was introduced to Paulo Freire's *Pedagogy of the Oppressed*. It was an assigned reading for the class Teaching Literature and Reading in Secondary Schools taught by Dr. Miller. The word oppression and its many forms were still quite new to my vocabulary. I was eager to read, consider, and apply this book to my teaching beliefs, but also to my life. I thought back to the kids that must have spent every day feeling miserable because they were not only taunted by their peers, but shut down in the classroom as well. I truly believe that motivating, empowering, and educating young people is vital for a better world. Freire's book gave me the theory, language, and tools to develop a social justice pedagogy that supported and strengthened my teaching beliefs and strategies. Dr. Miller, was enacting the work of Freire right in my college class. My classmates and I learned about projects we could use in our future classrooms, while Dr. Miller used strategies that promoted student voice and individuality. Dialogue was central to Dr. Miller's class, and it was very important for me to talk about issues or teaching strategies with my peers. Her classroom was an environment that allowed for free discussion. Dr. Miller made our class more conscious of the injustices in our society and schools, so it is now my responsibility to carry out such tasks in my future class-room.

Applications of Life to Teaching: sj

I recognize that our country has a history of prejudice and intolerance about anything that threatens the "moral" fabric upon which it was initially founded. At the same time that I experience a legacy of oppression daily whether it is when I walk down the street, see students clump together on campus for self-preservation, watch or read the news, listen to stories of friends who have been gay-bashed, or watch our country's leaders try to rewrite prejudice back into the Constitution, I know that I cannot enforce change through my teaching as that would be hypocritical, but I do know that I can live by example and can model respect and compassion. I am saddened when I see, learn about, or experience any type of covert or overt oppression and sometimes wonder if this is the way it will always be even with all of the positive changes that have been made to make our country more accepting and welcoming.

When I work with my preservice teachers and support inservice teachers who continue to write, email, and call with questions about their social and moral responsibility to address intolerance in school, I always respond with resources and follow-through. I am often plagued by the numbers of requests I receive and though I have never catalogued them, a majority have fallen around the rights of queer students and the mistreatment of urban students. Though I am not surprised that a majority of requests concern these students, it does alert me to how much more work we need to do in our preservice methods classes to try to eradicate prejudice and mistreatment.

This concern brings me to an area that the authors of this book addressed in the introduction—the efficacy that our social justice work has between university and secondary spaces. I am concerned that we are working with preservice teachers who are farmed to schools where they have little support to carry on their social justice work and may even be vulnerable to losing a job if they are too outspoken on a given issue. I remind myself that in spite of what may or may not happen in my students' placements, that I must be relentless in body, mind and spirit to not abandon what I believe are my social and moral responsibilities to cultivating and nurturing students who are prepared with the tools that can impact systemic change. I also know it is important to have heartfelt discussions with my students about where they teach and what some of the obstacles may be in certain school districts. As such, students must be the ones who ultimately make a choice about where they work. In order to best support a decision in the making, I encourage my preservice teachers to consider:

- "nondiscrimination laws" especially as they pertain to GLBT (gay, lesbian, bisexual, or transgender) teachers,
- how one's lifestyle may be affirmed or challenged in a particular school district and,
- how one's values (religion, the environment, politics, culture) and which kinds of schools and districts may challenge, affirm, or disaffirm them.

Regardless of some of the ways that prejudice continues to manifest in schools, I stay true to a course on teaching for social change. By welcoming feedback from former and current students like Channell and Kristy, I become better informed about the efficacy my university work has and if needed, can shift the conditions that I establish in my courses so as to meet the needs of my students.

Developing a Critically Conscious Social Justice Pedagogy

Throughout my years of teaching, I have come to understand how important it is for teachers to not only understand why they teach as they do but how it aligns with their belief systems. I believe that for learning to be engaging and for it to take on meaning in one's life, it must connect the spatial and the temporal. A goal I have in working with preservice teachers is to mentor them through a process of coming to terms with how they activate a pedagogy that not only works for them but also for their students. When individuals are able to align their belief systems with their professional goals, spiritual and emotional integrity follow. It is therefore critical that I offer opportunities that can help facilitate preservice teachers' spiritual growth so they embody a pedagogy that reflects their higher selves—this means teaching about a spectrum of pedagogies, regardless of my belief systems. Throughout a semester I model various pedagogies which include: monological, equity, behaviorist, engaged, literacy, hip-hop, critical hip-hop, performative, liberatory, feminist, queer, and transformative. Parker Palmer (1998) reminds us in *The Courage to Teach* that we must care for the heart of our teachers if true transformation is to occur because "good teaching cannot be reduced to technique; good teaching comes from the identity and integrity of the teacher" (p. 10).

In my methods courses I take my students through a journey that helps them explore their pasts, where and how their belief systems evolved, and how that manifests in their professional lives. This journey is threefold because in the process of supporting teachers come to terms with their pedagogies, they (1) come to understand how their biases impact their pedagogies, (2) discover how their pedagogies bridge to larger sociopolitical issues and social activism and, (3) discover how to select texts that best reflect the goals and objectives of their pedagogies. I always use Freire's *Pedagogy of the Oppressed* because it is a parallel path for many of my students to unveil how they have either been oppressed or participated in somehow, whether intentional or not, oppressing others. Freire is often difficult for students to digest and I first develop a context for students and then design and redesign activities that bridge Freire's work to their lives. Throughout the semester, I pace our reading of Freire as it aligns with issues in our lives and what is transpiring globally.

Supporting my students in developing a holistic identity, one that bridges the personal and the political, is not an easy feat. In fact, sometimes my evaluations suffer because I unpack too much personal history, or students who are resistant to liberatory learning, do not want to engage in class. Sometimes when students look into their pasts and see how they have been co-constructed by the matrix of family, friends, community, politics, social groups, faith, schooling, etc., it is not always rosy (Miller, 2005a). In fact, I recognize that there is resistance to participatory learning but use it is a touchstone to keep moving forward toward teaching about agency, transformation, and above all, personal empowerment. Freire (1970) tells us that a liberatory pedagogy seeks to educate students to act on and transform their worlds through acts of cognition first, and action, second. He suggests that when we adopt a liberatory pedagogy, two distinct changes will occur: "when the oppressed unveil the world of oppression and through the praxis commit themselves to its transformation," and "in which the reality of oppression has already been transformed, this pedagogy ceases to belong to the oppressed and becomes a pedagogy of all the people in the process of permanent liberation" (p. 54). When we teach about Freire's teachings, we can activate and motivate students to become agents capable of acting on and transforming their worlds. Although our students may not oppressed per se, they are embedded within a matrix that sustains a hegemonic power and which reinforces particular social values and morals. A liberatory pedagogy can prepare them to think critically about their worlds and provide them the tools to be informed citizens so that when they need to act, they know how (Miller & Norris, 2007, p. 189).

When discussing a critically conscious teaching pedagogy, it is critical that I assist students in bridging the body/mind split. So often, competing sociopolitical agendas compete for teachers to use their curriculum in their classrooms.

Unless teachers are taught to think critically about who is publishing a text, who the audience is, and who funds the company, teachers may blindly adopt a text that counters his/her belief system. A liberatory pedagogist cannot afford to blindly accept information, rather, a liberatory pedagogist must be actively involved in unpacking any material that comes onto school ground. When supporting teachers to develop a critically conscious teaching pedagogy we must help them understand that for the body and mind to be separate is to dismember the teacher. When teachers function from this place, the system has control. When a teacher operates from this place, they lack true agency. We therefore must strive to teach teachers to co-opt their identities and help them see that they are subjects, not objects capable of acting on and transforming their students' lives. By rupturing the notion that teachers are objects, we shift the status of teachers from subservient clones into transformational agents. Empowering teachers to develop a critically conscious teaching pedagogy is a radical act that disrupts binary relationships embedded within hegemony:

> Danielewicz (2001) says that teacher education programs should foster teacher identity development to the highest degree possible. In helping preservice teachers recognize their own identity co-constructions, they become more informed about their own subjectivities that can empower them to challenge being co-opted by hegemonic-based discourse and thinking. Recognizing that their own teacher identities are situated within a complex networked matrix of spacetime relationships can help them negotiate their identity co-constructions and help them relocate to spaces that stabilize and affirm their teacher identities. (Miller & Norris, 2007, p.18)

Since teachers are embedded within a vastly complex web of social, political, and cultural relationships, each of which influences either individually, collectively, or at their crossroads, the identity of the individual at any given point in time (Miller, 2005a, forthcoming 2008) and because English teaching is not an isolated profession nor immune to changes in policy at the international, national, state, and local levels, teachers' identities are vulnerable to shifts along with the profession. As a result of the shifting nature of our field and the multiple contexts in which teachers engage, teachers' identities will be reconstituted during the spacetime in which the identity is being constructed. Because of this complexity and the imminent whimsicality of change, it is difficult to understand how concurrent competing forces are impacting the preservice teacher. Therefore it is critical that the activities that we use in our methods courses challenge how subjectivities are not only co-constructed but give way to voice and provide opportunities for teachers to see into the overarching looking glass of the profession. An informed teacher is a teacher who is better able to challenge the body/mind split.

Activities to Activate a Critically Conscious Social Justice Pedagogy

In supporting teachers to come to understand how their biases impact their pedagogies, in my courses we collectively journey as a community into our pasts. I explain to them that our experiences shape our belief systems which shape our identities and what we think of certain issues affects how we behave. I begin with some basic terms that support us in delving into the different pasts we each have. We define terms such as prejudice, power, and oppression (I am hesitant to provide definitions here because they vary depending on context and bias). We look at different forms of oppression through the "ISMS," "words that become 'nouned' and are laden with pejorative connotations based on actual or perceived differences" (Miller, 2005b, p. 88). Examples of "ISMS" include but are not limited to:

- Able-bodiedism, based on physical abilities
- Ageism, based on age
- Anti-Semitism, based on a person's being Jewish or from a Semitic country
- Classism, based on social class
- Heterosexism, based on the belief that everyone should be heterosexual
- Lookism, based on appearance
- Racism, based on a person's race, ethnicity, or national origin
- Religionism, based on religion
- Sexism, based on gender
- Sizism, based on weight or height. (GLSEN, 2001)

We also look at hate crimes locally and nationally and at local and national hate crimes legislation so that they develop a context for the outcome of prejudice. Finally, with such awareness fostered how prejudice manifests in our lives, I introduce the dangers inherent in adopting a pedagogy that may be infused with prejudicial beliefs through the cycle of violence. The cycle begins with myths or misinformation, stereotypes, or a biased history. The cycle continues as myths are validated and reinforced by institutions, culture, media, family, religion, and friends and then become socialized into the cycle. With enough repetition, the misinformation and myths become truth and anything that differs is perceived as abnormal. The cycle concludes with a behavior that can be prejudiced, or oppressive, or even a hate crime (Miller, 2005b). It is my responsibility to step in and help teachers understand how to interrupt the cycle anywhere. With such concepts out on the table, we then approach various meanings of pedagogy. I defer to Danielewicz's (2001) book *Teaching Selves* whose masterful research on pedagogy maps out concepts about different aspects of pedagogies. I do my best to help students understand that pedagogy is a combination of the theories that undergird the structural and performative aspects of the how and why they select materials, teach and dialogue as they do, and that they must also be actively involved in interrogating their practice. I reemphasize that pedagogies should be fluid because they can be ineffectual in some spaces depending on the students. I help them understand that as we grow in space and time our pedagogies are also likely to adapt.

'Beliefed'-Identities

I conduct an exercise where I ask students to draw a line down the middle of a piece of paper and create two columns. Atop the left column, students write "beliefs about students" and atop the right column they write "teacher identity." After students fill in their beliefs about students, they move to the left column and fill in how those beliefs affect how they would teach students. This activity can be conducted a number of different ways with filling in "beliefs about..." and then parallel it to a particular type of identity. We then share our answers which becomes a way for me to assess what kind of issues need to be addressed during the spacetime of that course. If I recognize that there is bias, prejudice or even overt oppression, I reconsider how to move forward carefully so that students can come to terms with how some of their beliefs may come across as prejudice to their students. During successive classes I carefully model different pedagogies and actively engage students in before and after exercises and give them opportunities to write and reflect on how a particular pedagogy was or wasn't engaging for them and whether or not it aligned with their belief systems. The main project for the course is to write a before and after pedagogy with revisions along the way. The assignment reads:

> Throughout the semester you will learn about the different aspects of developing a pedagogy. You are expected to keep careful notes about how and what causes shift in your thinking. Keep all of those details in your reflexive journal because your final project will be a meta-reflection on your pedagogy and how you came to develop it. At the end of the semester, you will present your final pedagogy and describe how your pedagogy shifted over the course of the semester, reading excerpts from the beginning and reflecting on those changes.

The process is typically rewarding for students and is an excellent check-in for me about how they grown in their thinking throughout the semester. I collect their pedagogies and carefully reflect on them so that I can adapt and shift conditions in my teaching if students seem to lack elements of social justice in their pedagogies. It is also important feedback if a student lacks a consideration for social justice in a pedagogy. I cannot enforce social justice in their pedagogieal maps and it would be contrary to social justice teaching if I required it. So instead, I look for reflection and support of their thinking. The best I can offer are tools that they can use in any situation that they might deem oppressive and I hope that over time they will access some of the learning from my courses.

Ultimately, all I can do is transact knowledge, skills, and love, and support teachers in being their best in the classrooms, freed of oppressive structures and thinking.

The Ways We Oppress

A second activity I engage my students in so that I can strengthen their stances on particular social justice issues is to have them to a quick write of about fifteen minutes whereby they answer these questions: describe a time when I was oppressed and how that made me feel and describe a time when I overtly or inadvertently oppressed another and consider how that may have made the other feel. Afterwards, they pair up in teams and share their answers. This activity tends to be fairly emotional for students especially when they confront aspects of their lives that may be less than glamorous. I remind them that oppression manifests daily in schools and unless we unpack our own pasts, we may perpetuate issues through our discourse and teaching.

Level Playing Field

A third activity we do is the "*level playing field*," an activity that has been widely circulated around the country and can be accessed on the web. The activity demonstrates how some people are institutionally advantaged and privileged over others simply by their social class, birth right, age, gender, sexual orientation, ability, or ethnicity. Participants stand side by side along a centerline and move forward, backwards, or not at all, based on a series of questions that are asked. Eventually the participants are stratified and the activity comes to a close. I then raise a piece of paper up and say the closest person to me can have a job to show how some people are advantaged over others because of the privileges they were born with. It is critical to have a lengthy discussion at the end so participants have an opportunity to reflect on their position and to enable them to critique the questions orally and in writing. The activity generally elicits emotional responses as most people are not fully aware how they are or aren't privileged over others. My hope for students as they exit the activity is that they recognize that no field is level and that they must build bridges to connect with all of the their diverse students and their needs.

Allies

Unless we teach our students the significance of being an ally, invisibility becomes normalized. An ally is a person who stands up for or supports someone who is being oppressed and challenges oppression when, not if it happens. It has been my experience that sometimes people opt not to become an ally because it can position the individual as part of the group that is being targeted. My objective then is to explore with my students how to work through some of the fear they may carry around being an ally. It is therefore critical that we speak about the importance of being an ally in our methods courses. As an ally, we can help preservice teachers make a stand against oppression and prejudice in all forms and address concerns they may have early on simply by opening up dialogue. We can help them consider the benefits of being an ally and the significance of that in both their own as well as their students' lives.

The next activity we participate in is called caucusing which is meant to develop the concept of what it means to be or become an ally. For this activity students brainstorm on the chalkboard a list of various groups that are targeted in school. Once amassed, students volunteer to write one name of each one of the groups on a piece of butcher paper. As students move to their stations, I then say, write down all derogatory terms that are associated with those names. For instance, if one of the groups named is "queer students," some of the derogatory terms that may be written are "fag," "dyke," and "reject." Once the writer lists as many derogatory terms as possible, students rotate and add additional names to others' papers. After the rotation, students return back to their original group and then I say, "Please hold up your papers one at a time. These are the words that we never want heard in our classrooms or schools again. I ask you all to commit to standing up for any student or peer who is targeted." Then they read the terms aloud and talk. Although not an exhaustive list, groups generally fall around: band, drama, cheerleaders, nerds/geeks, techies, queers, jocks, skaters, and hippies.

Social Action Project

I encourage my students to make a stand about what is important to them in their lives. Whether this includes being a vegetarian, an environmentalist, a big-sister or big-brother, or a volunteer at a hospice, it is fundamental to their growth as humanitarians. As such, part of developing a critically conscious teaching pedagogy is about commitment to social action. An activity that I have my students partake in is first doing a social action project and then designing a social action project for their own students. The criteria are as follows:

For my students
Transforming Prejudice Project
You are to develop an action plan for your school environment.

Requirements:
- Identify an institutional or socio-cultural issue that students face in your school
- Discuss this issue with colleagues, peers, students, and school officials
- Decide on a way that you could work to help transform this issue into social activism within the school setting

- Describe the players involved, the results and the steps you could take in order to combat this particular issue
- Describe how this joint action could remain as a pillar in the school community (after you leave)
- Be sure to describe any theoretical perspectives/stances you apply to this action
- Paper must be typed with 10 or 12 pt font (preferably Arial or Times), spacing 1.5-2 in. Not to exceed 4 pages
  **Note— this project may be done with other student teachers in your cohort.

For their students—

Please include the following when designing your project.
- Name the project
- Articulate the purpose and your intent in creating such a project; i.e., how it might benefit students
- Clearly describe any concerns you might have in the project's execution up front.
- Develop set criteria for the project
- Provide a due date

Students generally enjoy this work immensely and it introduces or reintroduces them to their own agency in their schools. Students have been known to start different clubs as a result of this activity including a gay/straight/alliance, environmental/green club, peer-allies, and even a peer-tutoring for expectant mothers.

Channell's Inservice Teaching: Challenging Oppression in High School

Before I am able to cultivate an awareness for social justice amongst my students by discussing issues that they may not be emotionally prepared to handle, I have to look at the racial and cultural composition of my students, and carefully develop a reading curriculum that fosters the foundation to discuss issues in an objective manner. Students are not always willing to accept others' opinions that conflict with their own, so I feel that it is up to the teacher to create an environment within his or her classroom where students can participate in discussions that are focused on issues that are less controversial and emotional. With routine practice and thoughtful dialogue, students can become more capable of dealing with opposing ideologies and are more likely to engage in respectful disagreements instead of chaotic debates. Because many of my students and their families are originally from Mexico, it is easy for them to have a bias stance due to the negative image of their people that has developed within the United States. As their educational leader and mentor, I feel it is up to me to help them evaluate where their own personal biases come from, and who helped to shape them. It becomes very emotional because many realize how ignorant they have been, and that influential and valued family members have influenced some of the prejudices that have developed from within their own consciousness.

There is no specific lesson or technique, but rather an expectation to achieve an understanding of the importance of how hegemony exists and affects the belief systems of individuals and targeted groups. A majority of students that I interact with are not fully responsive to the fact that they too are influenced by specific individuals or ideologies that come from the media, religion, politics, etc. I find that it is not until my students begin to investigate what influences and shapes their beliefs, choices, and routine practices are they finally able to identify whose political or social agendas they are supporting. It is my intention to construct a system of belief that supports the need for awareness in the realms of social justice and equity in relativity to individuals from all identifiable groups. My students cannot become social activists for positive change in their communities until they are able to identify the oppression that exists. Many of them are too absorbed by how they are personally oppressed by others, and they act out by challenging these oppressors instead of trying to transform the process into a positive social change.

As a result of my schooling and teaching experience, I have adopted pedagogical practices which are liberatory and that incorporate both a behaviorist and transformative approach by evaluating specific behavioral patterns amongst my students, trying to understand from where these behaviors originated, identifying why they still exist, and contemplating how to transform the environment they exist in so that change is initiated from their own conscience. As an educator in this community of teachers and students, I have identified a crisis within the system that is not being addressed. This issue permeates all aspects of the objectives that the educational system serves, and until identified and discussed, the quality of public education will continue to deteriorate. This crisis that I have experienced in my three years of public school teaching is that I am not just trying to teach my immigrant students English reading, writing, and speaking skills, but that I am trying to teach them the culture of education. A majority of the student body does not see the value of an education because they are coming from a culture where working hard labor jobs are acceptable, honorable, and generational. I have conversed with many of my students about their goals. It is not that they do not have a dream to go to college; they do have the dream, but that is exactly what it is, a dream. The interfering factor that exists is that they have not been exposed to other individuals within their families who have attended a college or university and who have attained college degrees. I liken this to the idea that if someone has never tried filet mignon, then s/he may never understand it's possible exquisiteness. These students have never tasted the result and overriding benefits that come from achieving a higher education. They do not know any path that they could take to get to college, and once there, do not even know what skills they would need in order to succeed. They do not realize how necessary a post secondary education is at this point in their lives because they are not having to compete for decent paying jobs against other highly educated and qualified candidates; instead, they are witness to the daily economic struggles that their families incur at minimal paying jobs. One might think that because they witness their families' struggles that they would be more apt and determined to have an education so that they too would not have to struggle as their parents have but that is not the case. I do not have an easy answer here, but do believe that they lack this motivation to achieve a higher education due to the fact that they have not been exposed to close family members or friends that have embarked on the process of achieving this academic necessity and have not been witness to the intrinsic and extrinsic rewards and sense of accomplishment that comes with a college education. I ponder, how do we, as educators and community representatives, approach this transformation in a way that does not cause social grief from within the community and system?

There is one primary tension that exists in my school and local community. It is a division that exists between students who are from Mexico, and students who consider themselves local Hispanics. The controversial ideology that exists is one of invasion. There is a feeling of infringement that coincides with the belief that the Mexican population is below everyone else. They are limited to their Spanish language and choppy English fragments and are willing to take the jobs that are looked down upon; because of this, their race is looked down upon, and little is done to improve this situation. Paulo Freire (1970) explains that, "The oppressed, who have adapted to the structure of domination in which they are immersed, and have become resigned to it, are inhibited from waging the struggle for freedom so long as they feel incapable of running the risks it requires" (p. 47). It is territorial, and I believe that the local community is reacting more to the change in atmosphere and environment than to the people themselves. The south side of Santa Fe has transformed more than any other part of the city. It is in this area that the majority of the Mexican population resides, and it is in the northern, wealthier sector of the city that they work as construction workers, cashiers, dish washers and cooks at elite restaurants, and house cleaners. These are the jobs that one would expect the local high school and college students to be competing for, but because the Mexican population is more visible filling these positions, students feel like they are too good for these minimum wage occupations.

Another tension that exists is the fact that students who are limited to speaking primarily Spanish are placed in classes with English-only speaking teachers and students. With this type of environment, prejudice and physical division is bound to take place; I have seen it take place in my classroom. Mexican, bilingual students group together on one side of the room, and all others group on the other side. With the way my classroom is arranged with the students' desks in the shape of an oval, it sometimes looks like a scene from *Westside Story* with the Sharks and the Jets facing off. When I encountered this for the first time, I knew that I did not need to react to it immediately by bringing too much attention to the obvious situation, but rather, I went home and thought about a more effective way to address the physical environment of the classroom as to prevent this from taking place the next day. Unfortunately, there are many teachers that neglect to address situations like this because they too have their own racial and judgmental issues that they are not willing to compromise. It is difficult for everyone involved. I sympathize with both the mono and bilingual groups, but remain true to my own identity and beliefs by following my heart and by maintaining a personal philosophy that aligns with acceptance and empathy.

As a monolingual English-speaking teacher, I find myself frustrated and discouraged when I am trying to teach high school students how to write complete sentences, how to utilize punctuation, and how to spell basic monosyllabic words. The most frustrating observance that I make at the beginning of each new school year is the low reading levels of the students that enter my classroom. Classroom teacher and literacy specialist, Cris Tovani (2000), explains this blanket frustration by stating, "Few middle and high school teachers feel they have the time or the expertise to teach students how to read. They have been trained in their content area and are uncomfortable stepping into the role of reading specialist" (p. 13). The most common conversation with my colleagues that I have is about the low reading levels of our students. The conversation turns from frustration to accusation inquiring what the elementary and middle school teachers are doing if we are getting illiterates. The other problem is that we receive students who have very limited English skills because their families' primary language is Spanish. This is just a commonality amongst the majority of our students, and I feel that we, as educators, need to help our students grow academically as readers no matter how deficient they are. I realize that I am not only teaching my students how to write an essay or how to read a paragraph, but rather, how to take risks without the fear of ridicule and judgment. I tell my students that we all are continuously judged by others, and it is until we do not allow these judgments to shape who we are, that we can grow and become stronger.

I have found that by creating a nurturing and encouraging environment where issues surrounding social justice can be thoughtfully and respectfully discussed, my students are able to become more aware of how their beliefs have shaped who they are and how their social activism shapes those around them. It seems so elementary to state the golden rule, "do to others as you would like done to you," but it is very true, and I think about this when I find myself in a situation where I am wrongfully prejudging others. No one individual is capable of eliminating prejudice from his or her slate, but as long as one is conscious of the prejudgments that manifest from within, and there is an effort to correct them, then transformation can take place.

In my school community, the Mexican population of students is prominent. In my classes there is a large range of motivation. On one side of the spectrum, I have identified Mexican students that work extremely hard to achieve the best academic results that they can, and on the other side, students who sit passively without inquiring for help or students that act out in order to cover up their academic inabilities. My interest was spurred by the differences in these three cohorts of students and their academic potentials. For three years, I have maintained the position of coordinator for a college preparatory program at my school called AVID, an acronym that stands for "advancement via individual determination." This program was created twenty-five years ago in San Diego, California by an English teacher, Mary Catherine Swanson, who was baffled by the fact of how many of her academically able minority students neglected to challenge themselves by registering for honors and Advanced Placement courses. She created an elective class at her school that focused on minority students, first-generation college attendees, students who were academically "in the middle," those who were underrepresented in four-year colleges and universities, and for students with special circumstances who were individually determined to graduate and attend college. Within this elective class, she required her students to enroll in the most rigorous classes, and to support them, collaborative tutorial sessions were provided twice a week. She took them on field trips to nearby colleges and universities to expose them to the collegiate environment that could motivate them to continue to follow their dreams for a higher education. This was a program that was created when I was two years old, and I never thought that it would be the motivating factor that ignited the social justice factor in my teaching career to push my students beyond their proposed potential.

I took on the responsibility of teaching the AVID elective class my first year of teaching without realizing that I had been given the greatest opportunity that any teacher could ask for. I would be guiding a group of twenty-five academically motivated, not necessarily academically proficient students, as their AVID elective teacher throughout their four years of high school. It would be my responsibility to make sure that each one of them was on a rigorous academic and civic pathway toward his/her goals of graduating from high school, become leaders within their community, and ultimately attend college. Upon receiving and carefully evaluating their information sheets on the first day of school, I soon began to realize that more than ninety of these students were bilingual. I, along with the small percentage of students in the class that were not Spanish proficient like the others, were shocked, and needless to say a little intimidated by this factor. As their teacher and educational leader in the classroom, I felt like I would be facing a greater challenge than I ever thought possible. I immediately began to question my own ability to lead these students through four years of high school without being able to speak their native Spanish language. Would they accept me as their teacher? Would they value and trust the curriculum and strategies that I would bequeath upon them? It was this struggle that made me reevaluate my approach to teaching before I even began to teach. This is where I had to look at the social composition of the class and make adjustments. I knew that prejudice existed within the school against the Mexican population of students, but how would I eliminate and prevent it in my own classroom? It was this moment that I realized that I would strive towards social equity in my classroom in my pedagogy if I were to have any success with these students.

When I think about how social justice is entwined in my pedagogy, I have to look at who I am and how I connect or conflict with my students' individual needs. I am consciously evaluative of the curriculum that I propose and present to my students. I make sure that they are critical of what is being presented to them and for whom it benefits. I am constantly reflective on the approach I take when interacting with my students on relatively controversial issues, and how I allow them to interact with one another. Building positive and trusting relationships with my students is very important to me especially when it comes to emerging cultures. I have observed that no matter how effective a lesson may be, if I do not have the trust and respect of my students, learning will not take place. In *Affirming Diversity*, Sonia Nieto (2004) quotes Jim Cummins who states, "The interactions that take place between students and teachers and among students are more central to students success than any method for teaching literacy, or science, or math" (p. 330). I feel that it is not the lesson that makes students engaged, but the respect and devotion they have toward their teacher. If a solid, caring, trusting, and supportive relationship is developed between a teacher and his or her students, then that teacher can teach anything, and his or her students will commit to it, and immerse themselves in the value of it. My approach is a human approach; I am who I am, they are who they are, and I can function from that perspective as a teacher and as a member of my community. The difficulty is trying to embed, foster, and cultivate an air of acceptance, understanding, and empathy within a community of students who are constantly fighting for acceptance, and raging against the ignorance that exists everywhere they turn. It is a very difficult process to get my students away from the mindset of constantly feeling underrated, belittled, and oppressed. I have noticed that it

is not until my students are ready to be critical of themselves that we as a classroom community are finally able to discuss social injustices in an objective and
thoughtful manner.

It was the spring of 2006 that I faced a challenge that spurred a greater desire to enact an environment that focused on the social justice and injustices
that we as a school, community, and nation were facing more deliberately than
we ever had. Immigrant students and their families were in a state of fear and
emotional instability when the media delivered the news that political discussions were taking place in regard to the deportation of illegal immigrants to
their countries of origin. Up until that moment, I was negligent to the reality of
how many of my own students were undocumented immigrants and that their
lives were being placed in an emotional upheaval that I could never understand.
The fear and adolescent innocence displayed in their eyes, along with their sense
of desperation, catapulted me into a state of action. My students wanted to
speak out on behalf of all immigrants whether documented or undocumented,
but did not know how to approach the situation.

There was a mass cellular phone text message going around the nation that
had already been delivered throughout my school that all students were to conduct a "walk out" in response to the proposed legislation to dispose of all undocumented immigrants. As a United States citizen, I never thought that I
would be placed in a situation where I would be defending the livelihoods of
my students, their families, and millions of others who were undocumented
individuals within our country. Prior to these events, I had taken the stance that
immigrants need to enter our country through a process of legalization. I still
believe this; however, at that point in time, I was placed in a situation where I
had to reconsider my own belief system. I never imagined that I would be directly affected by this proposed legislation until my students confided in me
their status in this country along with the many horrifying stories of how they
and their families risked their lives to have the opportunity to live and work
here. Many of them looked at me with desperate eyes asking me, "Mrs. Segura,
do you think that this will really happen?" Many explained that their families
would be physically torn apart because even if they were legal, their parents
were not, resulting in them being separated from their parents and other family
members. Others expressed their frustration at the fact that their parents have
been trying for over ten years to become documented members of this country,
and have paid thousands of dollars, but to no avail. It all became emotionally
overwhelming for me to the point of breakdown, because some of my most
amazing, hard working students were undocumented. I never asked my students
to open up to me about their status in this country, but realized at that point the
trust that they had in me by voluntarily confiding in me. It was a waking point
for me to realize how much my students cared for and trusted me. It was then

that my beliefs were transforming because I realized the devastation that I too would experience if any of my students were deported.

When asked by my students if I would participate in the "walk out" with them, I did not know what to say. I knew that my students needed to voice their feelings on this conflicting issue, but I felt that a "walk out" of an educational institution would send our community the wrong message. By walking out of their classes, it did not need to be assumed that immigrant students did not value education, because many of them valued it equally if not more than many of the local citizens. Instead, I told my students that we were not going to participate in a destructive parade of degradation. I then spoke to my administrator about having an organized forum during lunch to allow students to voice their opinions whether for or against the controversial legislation. She hesitantly agreed to allow this realizing that it could result in a riotous situation. She and I deliberately invited the local media and law enforcement to participate in this forum as to not make it such a controversial event, but rather, an opportunity for students to voice their opinions. My students and I contacted the local immigration protection group, Somos Un Pueblo Unido, to assist us in projecting the facts of the legislation and the effects it could have on our country both locally and nationally.

This event resulted in two opposing groups shouting and waving Mexican and American flags at each other. Prior to the event that day, I had given my students the opportunity to discuss what conflicts and issues may arise out of this type of situation. It was an opportunity of growth for many of my students because at the end they all agreed that they needed to proud of where they came from and who they were by waving the Mexican flag, but also needed wave the American flag beside it to acknowledge the fact that the United States was now the country that they resided in and desired to remain in. In the end, many of my students who enacted their leadership skills so vigorously to arrange this event to be a positive outlet of organized discussions, were brought to tears with disappointment due to the dueling groups of students and teachers immaturely participating in shouting matches. I, as well as my students, used this as a learning experience and were enlightened to the ignorance and prejudice that was displayed by their peers as well as many of their teachers; my colleagues. It was obvious what my position was on this issue, and I still face colleagues who make it obvious that they do not want "aliens" in our school or in this country. It is a rude awakening, and it makes me question how far we have developed as a country to eliminate the hate and ignorance that color the canvas for the destruction of the human race. Overall, the experience and process that my students evoked, made them realize the power they had and their abilities to enact opportunities for social justice. The awakening that arose in me due to this event, as well as the priceless influence of my pre-teaching studies with my cooperative teacher, created a desire in me that has filtered into my teaching. I am now able and willing to full-heartedly approach with my students the importance and value of action in regards to social justice.

It is a difficult endeavor to make my students aware of the necessity to develop a critically conscious social justice stance, because it forces them to be reflective of their own prejudices and insecurities. In preliminary discussions on social issues, I have noticed that my students are very willing to supply their own opinions without thinking of how they may affect others in the group. It is not intentional; they are just naïve in regards to sensitivity factors that are present amongst their peers, and until genuine feelings are affected by the verbalization of their views and opinions, do they finally become conscious of themselves and others. It is a risk on any teacher's behalf to allow his or her students to discuss their viewpoints on certain social issues because no matter how much one tries to prepare and create a nurturing environment, feelings are sometimes evoked that are unintended.

Kristy's Preservice Teaching: Challenging Oppression in Middle School

As a culminating assignment for Dr. Miller's class, I wrote a teaching pedagogy. At that point in my teacher-training career, I knew the elements that I would need for a productive English classroom, and after reading Freire and completing Dr. Miller's class, I knew my pedagogy would also represent my stances on social justice issues. I intend to give students the tools to analyze all aspects of society. The four stages of critical literacy not only support the goals of an English curriculum, but promote and call for sociopolitical action. I have a need to help and teach young people, especially those who feel oppressed. I can do that as a teacher. Equality and respect among students and teacher are necessary in my classroom. As Freire suggests, I will meet this goal by taking an active participatory role in the classroom, just like students. I have worked very hard to dissolve the communication barrier that discourages students from voicing opinions when the teacher is present. Student journals have allowed me to connect with students and the issues that are happening in school and in their lives. Often times the dialogue from student journals was brought up in Paideia seminars. During student teaching, Paideia seminars were scheduled as a culminating activity for students, although a seminar could be used at any point in a unit. The day before the seminar, the students and I spend about ten minutes generating possible questions and topics for the seminar. I encourage students to read through their journals in order to refresh their memory of the issues and topics they wrote about. I ask students to decide if they have changed their mind on any of the issues since we have now finished the novel. The next day I arrange the desks in a circle. Once class begins, I display the list of questions and topics from the previous day, and I remind students of the seminar rules. Students maintain the conversation, and I am the recorder. I remind them that they must be respectful of opinions and give everyone the opportunity to speak. Usually, it is awkward for students at first but with time students really like seminar because they realize they control the conversation, and I trust them to lead the class. The seminars really helped my classes to understand that they could discuss important issues amongst themselves, proving they could do the same outside the classroom. When students discussed Tolan's, *Plague Year* I was impressed by their discussion. They spent time discussing the definition of a true friend, and the moral dilemmas in the novel.

During my student teaching experience, I was fortunate enough to have the opportunity to address the issue of bullying. The first unit I was to teach revolved around the novel, *Plague Year*. After reading the novel on my own I was very excited because it was a perfect opportunity to examine bullying both in school and within community. The novel takes place in a small rural town. The main character, Bran Slocum is immediately taunted and bullied because of his style of dress and his physical traits. Molly, another student who is often taunted for her appearance and personality, befriends Bran. Molly introduces Bran to her only friend, David. David is a popular student, who would rather not be seen with Bran, but with time he looks beyond Bran's appearance. Members of the town learn that Bran's father is the suspect in several murders which is the reason for Bran moving to town. This accusation gives the bullies at school and the townspeople more reason to torment Bran. Although the novel is harsh at times and some minor characters are stereotypical, the events in the novel make students question the definition of friendship, address bullying and the treatment of people.

My cooperating teacher and student teaching supervisor encouraged me to develop lesson plans that would address the issue of bullying. With resources from www.teachingtolerance.com, I developed a lesson plan that surveyed students about their experience with bullying. If the student answered "yes" to the question they wrote the question number on a red slip of paper. If they answered "no" to the question they wrote the question number on a blue slip of paper. I displayed the results of each class period on the board. If the visual effect of the colors was not astonishing enough, the percentages were. A large percentage of students admitted that they had experienced harsh bullying, and a large percentage admitted they had been guilty of bullying. When second period walked into the classroom and I raised the cover to display the results, silence covered the room as the students took in the numbers. After a few minutes group of students tried to make excuses for the shocking results; however, the previous day they indeed were taking the survey very serious.

The survey results developed into a very productive and proactive discussion about bullying in their school. Several members of the administration came to the class and listened in on the discussion. I remember when the principal walked into my second period class the day of my bullying lesson plan. After the initial shock of realizing my class and I were going to be observed, I quickly transitioned to the survey results and waited for students to respond. The principal stood in the back of the class with my cooperating teacher just staring at the red and blue slips of paper displayed on the board. My cooperating teacher later told me the principal said, "I am speechless. The responses bring tears to my eyes." Before the principal left the room she voiced her support of the school anti-bullying policy and told students that they are surrounded by people, who will help them when they are faced with issues. I had succeeded at making my point and helping students to speak about an important social and school issue.

Besides direct thematic units, there are several ways that my social justice pedagogy worked in my student teaching classroom and will work in my own classroom. Almost every day, students had time to freewrite. I would often provide students with writing prompts or quotes which usually worked to draw out their opinion on the topic. I encouraged students to share their writing in small groups as well as with the entire class. I always tried to choose writing topics that pertained to their lives or a topic that would ignite opinions. For example during the unit on *Plague Year,* I asked students to respond to the following writing prompt: "Do you judge people based on their family and friends? Why or Why not? If Bran Slocum's father is evil person, who lacks respect for the lives of others, is that reason to avoid or hate Bran?" Students found they had mixed feelings on the question, and needed to verbally discuss their responses as a group. I responded to their journal entries, if they indicated they wanted me to. Students were always very eager to read my response and often would eagerly want to talk after class. One student wrote a lengthy response to the above prompt. She said that she felt as though teachers judged her based on her last name. She has an older brother, who is a struggling student and brings discipline issues to the class. Because she feels some teachers immediately label her "a bad kid" she often doesn't participate and barely completes the work. We talked about her response and some possible ways she could try to boost her confidence in other classes.

Dialogue is a major fact in my classroom. I want students to understand that their opinion and voice matters in my classroom as it does outside in the community and world. I also hope to develop a social justice unit where students go out into the community and devise a plan to improve some aspect of the community or raise awareness on an issue. I always think back to the documentary, *Paper Clips*, a documentary about a project initiated by the principal of Whitwell Middle School, a small rural school in Tennessee. She wanted to educate her students and the community about diversity of the world outside of

Whitwell. The documentary shows the progression of students as they learn about the Holocaust, the intolerance, and the loss of life that surrounded it. The students and teachers organized a campaign to collect one paper clip for each life lost in the Holocaust. The eleven million paper clips are now displayed in a railcar that was once used to transport victims. I first saw the film in Dr. Miller's class. I was sitting in an uncomfortable wooden desk surrounded by my classmates. While I watched the movie my eyes periodically filled with tears. At first, I hoped people didn't notice the tears, but I realized I was weeping for many reasons and it had to do with teaching, my persona, and everyone around me. I was weeping because I was being reminded of the intolerance and horrible conditions the people of the Holocaust endured; however, I was also teary eyed because the students and teachers in the film were a community with a goal to teach others to fight intolerance and remember those who suffered. At one point in the documentary a few of the middle school students were giving tours of the memorial and I noticed how proud they appeared as they guided visitors and yet it was the same kind of confidence and pride I noticed early in the film when students were packing request envelopes and opening donations—what might be perceived by some as a seemingly mundane task here, had great significance to everyone involved in the project. I think watching the documentary would empower students to address an issue and educate others.

Conclusion

sj

When students leave my courses, my hope is that they will leave more informed than when they arrived, be more willing to engage in social activism, and that their pedagogies reflect who they are and what they will embody and activate in the classroom. It has been my experience that when we re-read or re-teach, we can always finding something new but only if we have grown since the last reading or teaching is that possible and it is my desire that my pedagogy remains adaptive to whatever changes occur in education and society at large so that I can best meet the needs of diverse learners and thinkers. Both Channell and Kristy's experiences enacting social justice over space and during different times in their classrooms re-motivate me to continue to advocate for all students regardless of where they are farmed to teach.

Channell's Closing Words

As an advocate for social justice activism, I am placing myself in a compromising position due to the environment that I choose to work. I work for the public school system; a flawed system of rules and regulations, budget deficits, sometimes unattainable academic benchmarks and standards, low pay, and demanding expectations. Even though I can try to alleviate myself from this formalistic and functionist environment by participating in liberatory instruction and curriculum development, I am still hostage to an unrealistic agenda that lacks support, guidance, and explanation.

When I introduce the idea of social justice to my students and explain how important it is to advocate for themselves and their beliefs, I observe a sense of empowerment that did not exist in them before. It is a very touchy issue because I can not expect that all of my students are going to embrace this ideology. Even though many of them entertain the idea, and realize that they have always participated in some sort of social justice intentionally or unintentionally, there are those who exist that are insistent on maintaining their judgmental beliefs against others who are different from who they are. With these students, I do not push the issue, because it is not my job to make sure that all my students become advocates for social justice; instead, it is my job to make sure that they are all socially aware of the effects and repercussions of prejudice and discrimination.

Throughout my experience in the teaching profession, I have observed a lack of social justice as a component in any subject's curriculum. I have, and continue to juxtapose it with Socratic seminars, novels, writing, and projects. It is a sensitive issue, but I have found success in projecting myself as an equal to my students. I find that it is important to not try to pretend that I have all of the answers to anything that I teach, because I know that I do not. I consider myself a student who is always learning. Educator and author, Nancy Atwell (1998) explains, "Best means learning—and admitting—when I'm wrong" (p. 4). There is so much power and respect gained, when a teacher is able to permit him or herself to be human and admit to being wrong or not knowing certain information. I always assumed that my teachers knew everything about the subjects that they taught, but now that I am an English teacher, I am aware of the lack of knowledge that I have even having attained two college degrees. I am clear about my need to pursue continual professional development by taking more college classes, attending annual conferences, and collaborating with my colleagues to be the most effective educator that I can be for the benefit of my students and my own sanity. Because of this, I can walk into my classroom and allow myself to be on a semi-equal playing field with my students. I say "semi" due to the fact that I recognize my role in the classroom to be that of a leader, teacher, mentor, advocate, and mother; my students look up to me for guidance and good judgment and I know that I have these abilities to lead them all in the most successful directions.

It is true that the ideologies that make up the public educational system sometimes make it difficult to comply as an instrument within the system, but an educator who is willing to avoid this oppressive functioning can be very effective in the lives of many individuals who are starving for knowledge of fundamental social and academic skills, acceptance, and love. There have been many efforts to liberalize schooling by giving students and teachers more curricular freedoms and choices which include efforts to educate students on the importance of social justice, but ultimately, the traditional functionalist guidelines of teaching continue to prevail within this power hierarchy. Schools seem to merely function as sorting machines of inequalities that prepare students for the needs of the local economy. Bowles and Gintis (1976) discuss this problem by stating that:

> A major element in the integrative function of education is the legitimation of preexisting economic disparities. Thus efforts to realize egalitarian objectives are not simply weak; they are also, as we shall demonstrate, in substantial conflict with the integrative function of education. Ideologies and structures which serve to hide and preserve one form of injustice often provide the basis of an assault on another. The ideology of equal educational opportunity and meritocracy is precisely such a contradictory mechanism. (pp. 102-103)

As teachers, we need to challenge this oppressive functioning by emphasizing social justice activism, and by targeting all students, not just the students that demonstrate acceptance and academic potential, as individuals who are capable of competing in a market that requires more than a high school diploma. If we give up on the students who are ignorant, lack motivation, and not try to illuminate their existing potentialities, then we are just instruments within the institution supporting its oppressive functioning.

I believe that human transformation is inevitable because we live in an ever changing world. I am an educator because I believe in the power of transformational growth. Social justice is not something that is taught, but rather, it exists in the individual embedded deep within morality, civility, and an authentic belief in equity. There are many layers that surround this complex form of activism. For many, it is an awakening that does not occur until they find themselves, or someone they love and or respect, victims of social oppression. If I can prepare my students for the critical world that they are about to embark upon by educating them on issues that are relevant to their lives, by teaching them how be critical thinkers, and by helping them develop a strong sense of confidence so that they can advocate for themselves and those around them, then I feel that I have done myself justice in my own personal and professional experience as an educator.

Kristy's Closing Words

I have set my goals very high, and I intend to continue to entwine social justice into my teaching and life. It is simply the way I view the world and the people around me. I cannot overlook serious problems that are happening in our schools and society. As a teacher I can definitely help to make a change, even if it is just giving students the tools to analyze a political speech or help someone who is struggling. Despite all the positives and hopefulness, I know that I will always bump up against people who would rather not stir up issues. It is uncomfortable for most people to confront issues that threaten social justice. Based on my experience thus far, rural communities are resistant to examining social justice issues. It seems like many believe it is a problem someone else in a larger school system should address and solve. In rural school teaching, I know that I will need a sound rationale for teaching what I teach. I also think there is the possibility that my colleagues may not accept or support a social justice pedagogy because of long-entrenched history that predates such shifts in peda-gogical approaches. Even my mother as a special education teacher, has diffi-culty accessing necessary supports and resources for her students in a rural school district. If teachers are resistant to students who are legally entitled to certain things; imagine how some teachers may react when I'm letting my stu-dents make classroom rules and design their own projects that pertain to the community? A month or two after I completed student teaching, I was working as a substitute teacher in the same building. After class, an eighth grade girl walked up to me and said, "Can I ask you a question? There are three boys who stand in front of my locker each day. They call me the same names over and over, and they won't let me get to my locker. I think that is considered bullying. Are you able to do something about it?" I notified the assistant principal, and the boys were questioned and reprimanded. Almost three months later the bul-lying lesson plan truly came around full-circle. I realized that I had raised aware-ness and empowered at least one student to stand up. It is a consummate example why I hope to always maintain a social justice pedagogy.

Fourthspace Embodied by Channell and Kristy

Both Channell and Kristy have discovered for themselves the true, existen-tial importance of enacting a pedagogy with social justice at its core. They have both struggled with colleagues, other students, and even within themselves to stand for others in the face of adversity because of systemic problems that are deeply entrenched in our country and the educational systems in which they each teach. Some of the personal and professional work they have encountered has been relegated to fourthspace (the space where power can neither be usurped nor exhausted) because they have had to disguise some of their own feelings in fear of retribution; as in Channell's case about the "walk out" and wanting to stand with her students, or as in Kristy's case, tip-toeing to find people who would support her in teaching a unit on bullying and social activ-ism. Nonetheless, they have each in their own ways, discovered for themselves, the how and the why they must keep social justice at the core of their beings. Such acts has demanded from each of them, indomitable courage.

I suspect that both Channell and Kristy will always carry a newfangled passion for social justice teaching into any space they might teach because they have been able to embody and sustain the personal and institutional identities of social justice teaching, and because they have each been able to connect social justice to many discourses in their lives. On this Gee (1992) says, when we live something, we can become something. I do not think, however, that this would be the case for any preservice teacher just coming into a career. I believe that just as a child needs guardians to support them developmentally by scaffolding their social, emotional, physical/corporeal and cognitive development, so too, do inchoate and even inservice teachers require a developmental model that can facilitate, cultivate, develop and sustain them in their social justice teaching identity over time and in different spaces. Therefore, more longitudinal research needs to address how social justice identities can be cultivated and institutionalized during different spacetimes.

I propose that we consider how fourthspace can serve as a conceptual framework for scaffolding social justice pedagogy and identity development into preservice teaching. This would mean developing, nurturing, and embedding the emotional and corporeal responses around social justice issues so that preservice teachers embody both a social justice pedagogy and identity. Gee's (2002) model on identities as analytic tools for understanding schools and society provides sound rationale for such an approach. He suggests that identities are dialogical and relational, constructed in relation to power, and are constructed in relationship to discourse. He also says that individuals have multiple and even hybrid identities which are intercontextually malleable and consequently, ever-changing, and readily influenced by space and time. Such identities can be categorically and multiply assigned to:

- *nature-identity*, N-identity (that which develops biologically and in nature)
- *institutional-identity*, I-identity (that which is influenced by institutions),
- *discourse-identity*, D-identity (that which is developed relationally to others), or
- *affinity-identity*, A-identity (that which develops in relation to participation in a group or community).

If we consider social justice as an identity that can be an analytic lens to view schools and society which one comes to embody over time and through intercontextual participation, then it can be assigned as an I, N, and D-identity and perhaps over time, an A-identity. Once such a model is in place, we can begin to expand on some of these initial concepts as expressed in the 5 "re-s." Then perhaps over time, identity and social justice pedagogy may even blend into one in the same and become a mainstay in teacher education. Perhaps in time, and with furthered activism around social justice research, a fourthspace may not be needed to disguise or "protect" our preservice teachers from freely expressing themselves in their schools. I maintain the hope that we can arrive at a point in the schooling of youth where social justice becomes an inherent part of our curricular objectives and our teachers can enact a true sense of democracy without fear of retribution.

References

Atwell, N. (1998). *In the middle: New understandings about writing, reading, and learning.* Portsmouth: Boynton/Cook.

Bowles, S., & Gintis, H. (1976). *Schooling in a capitalist America: educational reform and the contradictions of economic life.* New York: Basic Books.

Danielewicz, J. (2001). *Teaching selves: Identity, pedagogy and teacher education.* Albany: State University of New York Press.

Freire, P. (1970). *Pedagogy of the oppressed.* New York: Continuum.

Gee, J. (1996). *Social linguistics and literacies: Ideology in discourses* (2nd ed.). New York: Falmer Press.

———. (2002). Identity as an analytic lens for research in education. In W.G. Seceda (Ed.), *Review of research in education* (Vol. 25)(pp. 99-125). Washington, DC: AERA.

GLSEN Terms. (2001). *An Anti-Homophobia, Prejudice-Reduction Curriculum* [Nonpublished document]. Santa Fe: GLSEN/Santa Fe Rape Crisis Center.

Level Playing Field. (2001). *An Anti-Homophobia, Prejudice-Reduction Curriculum* [Nonpublished document]. Santa Fe: GLSEN/Santa Fe Rape Crisis Center.

Miller, S. (2005a). *Geographically "meaned" preservice secondary language arts student teacher identities.* Ann Arbor, UMI Dissertation Publishing, www.lib.umi.com/dissertations/fullcit/3177097.

———. (2005b). Shattering images of violence in young adult literature: Strategies for the classroom. *English Journal, 94*(5), 87–93.

Miller, s. (forthcoming, 2008). (Re)/Re-envisioning preservice teacher identity: Matrixing methodology. In J. Flood, S. B. Heath, & D. Lapp (Eds.), *Handbook of research on teaching literacy through the visual and communicative arts* (Vol. II). Mahwah: Lawrence Erlbaum Associates.

Miller, s., & Norris, L. (2007). *Unpacking the loaded teacher matrix: Negotiating space and time between university and secondary English classrooms.* New York: Peter Lang.

Nieto, S. (2004). *Affirming diversity: The sociopolitical context of multicultural education* (4th ed.). Boston: Pearson Education,.

Palmer, P. J. (1998). *The courage to teach.* San Francisco: Jossey-Bass.

Paper Clips. (2004). Dir. Elliot Berlin and Joe Fab. Prod. Joe Fab, Robert M. Johnson and Ari Daniel Pinchot. DVD. One Clip at a Time, HMA, and Slowhand Cinema.

Tolan, S. (1991). *Plague year.* New York: Random House.

Tovani, C. (2000). *I read it, but I don't get it.* Portland: Stenhouse.

6

Lifting the Veil of Ignorance: Thoughts on the Future of Social Justice Teaching

Todd DeStigter

"I would prefer not to."
Herman Melville's Bartleby the Scrivener

"Aw, hell no, Todd."
Mondale Johnson, Chicago high school student

About four years ago, the financial status of Latino Hope Alternative High School (a pseudonym), a small school of about 100 students located in Chicago's predominantly Mexican and Mexican-American community of Little Village, had become grave. Having been at Latino Hope for several years, first as a tutor and researcher, and by that time as a teacher of one of its daily English classes and a member if its board of directors, I had seen firsthand the unhappy effects of the school's dwindling resources. In science classes, for lack of equipment and materials, the teacher and students talked about experiments rather than actually doing them. A social studies teacher brought from home a small TV and DVD player so he could show the civil rights documentary *Eyes on the Prize* (which he had borrowed from the public library) in his U.S. History class. English teachers spent their own money on paperback books or went to Kinko's to make photocopies when the office copier broke down. Things had gotten so bad that on Friday afternoons, faculty and staff hurried to the bank after school to deposit their payroll checks for fear they would bounce.

It was at this point that the Executive Director of the social service agency that housed Latino Hope proposed a solution to the school's financial emergency. The Chicago Public Schools (CPS) had initiated a "Safe Schools Program," which removed from regular community schools students who were guilty of serious disciplinary offenses like gang membership, taking drugs or a weapon to school, and frequent fighting. These students, however, depending on their age, were still required to attend school or eligible for a public education, so the CPS offered a sizable amount of money to alternative schools for accepting them. The Executive Director's idea was to enroll at Latino Hope enough "safe school" students that the money that accompanied them—a quarter of a million dollars—would stabilize the school's finances.

This proposal, though practical enough, was highly controversial among the Latino Hope board members. Latino Hope had been established over thirty years before with its immediate community in mind, and its mission statement clearly stated that its aim was to provide an education and support services to Latino young people from Little Village. Throughout its history, that's exactly what Latino Hope had done, and with considerable success. In the four years I had spent at the school, I'd talked to scores of Latino Hope students who had dropped out or been expelled from other Chicago schools, and almost all of them preferred Latino Hope, saying things like, "Everybody's Mexican here, and a lot of them speak Spanish," or "Here the teachers know you and care about you." That is to say, students valued their experience at Latino Hope because it was a community based in large part on close personal relationships and a diverse but shared Latino identity.

The new "safe school" students, in contrast, would come from all over the city, thus introducing to Latino Hope an ethnic and racial diversity unprecedented in the school's history. Some board members strongly opposed the move, arguing that the school had a moral obligation to continue to provide a hospitable space for Latino students that they had not found in their previous schooling. Latino Hope had always been a place where many people could speak students' first language (Spanish), where they could get help with translation, where they could learn about their history and the struggle for Latino/Chicano rights, where who they were was valued and supported. To preserve this space, these board members asserted, was simply and obviously the right thing to do. However, other board members argued, equally convincingly, that the school's previous successes should not be restricted to Latino students, that all young people, regardless of their race or ethnicity, were entitled to the close attention and sense of kinship afforded by Latino Hope, and that to bar non-Little Village residents from membership in this school community for no reason other than the color of their skin would clearly be unjust.

I had come to know the Latino Hope board members as thoughtful, intelligent people who throughout their careers as business owners, public servants, and educators had demonstrated their commitment to justice for Latino Hope students and, more broadly, for the residents of Little Village—a shared sense of purpose that enabled us to reach consensus on most matters set before us. On this particular issue, however, the board was evenly divided, and after several meetings and long, sometimes contentious conversations, we were forced to put the matter to a vote. In the end, by one ballot, the board accepted the Executive Director's recommendation that Latino Hope begin accepting up to twenty-five "safe school" students. Mondale Johnson was one of those students, and the following fall term, he was enrolled in my second-period section of "English Three" (all names of people in this chapter are pseudonyms, except mine).

Latino Hope and Mondale

Mondale was a big kid, over six feet tall and weighing in, I guessed, at about 220 pounds. When he walked down the narrow corridor toward our third-floor classroom at the end of the hall, back lit by the glow of a window behind him, he appeared as a giant silhouette, swaying from side to side as much as he moved forward. Even without looking, I could tell from my classroom when Mondale was approaching because the hardwood floorboards creaked more loudly for him than they did for anyone else. Dressed, as he usually was, in a shiny sweat suit top, baggy jeans, and big, unlaced sneakers, because of his size Mondale would have been an imposing figure were it not for his round, boyish face. His dark skin was so smooth that it shined, and he wore his hair in tight corn rows tied at the ends with brightly-colored beads. Though Mondale seemed crabby most days, his mouth and brow often fixed in a scowl, when he smiled, when his eyes got big and he flashed his movie-star teeth, it was like someone had walked into the room and turned on the light.

I was joined in teaching English Three by a new graduate student, Nancy, who had taught in a Nebraska high school for several years before moving to Chicago to enroll in the university where I work. Nancy and I had met several times before the beginning of the semester to make plans for English Three, and I had been impressed by her intelligence and her commitment to teaching for social justice, which we agreed included helping students develop their literate potentials in ways that would enable them to exercise a wide range of choices in their lives and to pursue goals that they had reason to value. And so in crafting our syllabus, Nancy and I had deliberately drawn guidance from educational luminaries whose conceptual and ethical frameworks have been among the foundations of teaching for social justice for at least two generations. From Paulo Freire (1970/2002) we took a priority of eschewing "banking methods" of education in favor of "problem-posing" ones that begin with students' experience, raise critical consciousness, and create dialogue that empowers both students and teachers to become, as Freire puts it, "more fully human" (p. 44). From John Dewey (1916/1985) we took his emphasis on establishing our classroom as a community in which individual students could develop their unique potentials, welcome exposure to a wide range of associations, and discover common interests with others—all with the aim of enabling students to participate fully in the planning, implementation, and consequences of their activity (pp. 92-93). And from Maxine Greene (1988) we took an emphasis on the arts to help students imagine a better world and then work together on collective projects that would make that world a reality (p. 126).

More specifically, and guided by these priorities, Nancy and I included in our plans readings by and about Latino, African-American, and urban young people; we provided opportunities for a lot of in-class reading and writing to accommodate what we knew were the heavy after-school work schedules of most Latino Hope students; and we designed inquiry-based research projects (Fecho, 2004) that we hoped would encourage students to investigate the causes and consequences of conditions in their communities and then to act to either sustain or revise those circumstances as they saw fit. In this way, Nancy and I hoped to encourage our students to engage in *praxis*—reflective action directed toward making the world a more humane and just place than it is now (Freire, 1970/2002).

The first day of English Three, Mondale walked into our small classroom and squeezed into the seat nearest the door. He was one of two African-American students in the class, the other being his friend and cousin, Justin. The dozen other students, all of them Latino and most of whom I knew from previous semesters, settled into their seats. After going around the room and introducing ourselves, Nancy and I passed out and began to read a summary of what we had planned for the term, along with a list of "class expectations" that talked about fostering "community" by doing things like showing up for class on time and not talking over others. Throughout all this, Mondale was leaning forward, his arms on the desk, his head resting on his biceps. Near the end of the introduction sheet, Mondale suddenly got up and dragged his desk out the door and into the hallway just outside the classroom. Nancy and I looked at each other. I could tell she was waiting for me to respond, but I didn't know what to do. Should I ignore Mondale? Should I insist that he put his desk back into the room? What if he refused? But I couldn't just let him sit there, could I? What if he decided to move even further down the hall, or get up and leave the school altogether and just wander the streets? As his teacher, I was, after all, responsible for his safety. And what if the other students decided to leave, too? I stood there and pondered these questions, hoping that somehow I'd make a decision that would help foster a positive learning environment for everyone, a space where we could work together on our aims of social justice. But what that decision should be, I wasn't at all sure.

After an awkward moment, I asked Mondale if he was feeling okay. "Yeah," he said. I then asked him to bring his desk back into the classroom, trying to make light of it, saying something like, "We'll miss you if you're out there all by yourself." Mondale wasn't having any of it. Slouching, he said, "Naw, I don't want to be in there." I could feel Nancy and the other students watching me, again wondering what I would do. I wondered the same thing. I decided to try playing my authority trump card and insist that Mondale return to the room. "Okay, Mondale," I said, "it's distracting and, frankly, a little weird to have you sitting out there in the hallway. Please bring your chair back in here." Mondale responded by casually scratching his head, glancing down the hallway, and saying, "Aw, hell no, Todd."

On the page Mondale's response seems confrontational, like he uttered it while raising himself in his chair glaring at me. But that wasn't the case at all. Mondale's tone was placid, as if a friend had said to me, "No, thank you. I don't care for another cup of tea," or "Oh, that's not necessary, I'll just take the bus home." In the end, I figured as long as Mondale stayed where he was just outside the door, I could keep an eye on him and make sure he didn't wander off and get into trouble. Besides, none of the other students seemed inclined to leave. So I just said, "Okay," and went on with what Nancy and I had planned for the day.

Over the next several weeks, English Three settled into what Nancy and I thought was a satisfactory, even pleasant, routine. It's not that we didn't have any difficulties or setbacks along the way. Robert complained that we "never learned anything" in English Three because all we did, in Robert's words, was to "read all this stuff and then talk and write about it"; Candice was struggling to get caught up with her assignments after she had missed about a week of classes when her babysitter was sick; at the beginning of nearly every class, it took a minute or two of negotiation to get Juan to put away his personal stereo. Still, although most students seemed interested and engaged in what Nancy and I planned for each day, those students didn't include Mondale. He would do some of the work Nancy and I assigned, but if it didn't interest him, he'd sit quietly and read his copy of the *Sun Times*. Though he was, to me, unsettling in his unpredictability, his one constant was that each day he would show up on time for class and drag his desk into the hallway just outside the classroom door. I tried to talk to him about it, tried to convince him to join our class, which, in my view, seemed to be gelling nicely into a democratic "community" in the Deweyan sense of the word: that is, as a space where individuals "participate in an interest so that each has to refer his own action to that of others" (1916/1985, p, 93). Several times before or after class, I implored him to be reasonable, to consider the difficult position he put me in. "What if other students decide that they want to move their chairs out into the hallway?" I asked. "How would it be fair of me to allow you to do it but not let anyone else?" Mondale just shrugged, like that wasn't his problem. Most times that I asked him directly to reconsider, to join the group and make the most of what his classmates, Nancy, and I had to offer, he'd say the same thing: "Aw, hell no, Todd."

One day during class, about a month into the semester, after once again failing to convince Mondale to come in from the hallway, I sighed and leaned my head against the black board, smearing in a couple of places the instructions I had just written there. When I turned around, Candice raised her hand and motioned for me to come closer. "Todd," she said.

"Yes, Candice?"

"You got chalk on your forehead."

Mondale as "Bartleby"

Though I was able to get rid of the chalk dust with a swipe of my shirt sleeve, Mondale stayed on my mind. Nancy and I talked about him most days after class, and I was beginning to fear that I was letting her down. She had, after all, come hundreds of miles to Chicago to learn about educating for democracy and social justice, and I, with my feckless attempts at teaching Mondale, wasn't turning out to be a much of a mentor. After one such conversation, I went home and reread a story that, until recently, I hadn't thought much about since I first encountered it decades ago in an undergraduate American literature class: "Bartleby the Scrivener" by Herman Melville. For those unfamiliar with the story, "Bartleby" is narrated by a moderately successful Wall Street lawyer, who adds to his small office staff a "pallidly neat, pitiably respectable, incurably forlorn" copyist named Bartleby (p. 1332). At first the lawyer is pleased with Bartleby's laconic industry, but on the third day of Bartleby's employment, when the narrator calls his new scrivener to his office to proofread some documents, Bartleby calmly replies, "I would prefer not to." Bartleby's response sets in motion a series of events that at once exasperate and mystify his employer. The lawyer at first forgives Bartleby's eccentricities, but when Bartleby soon declares that he "would prefer not to" do any work at all, then is found to be living in the law offices after hours, then unnerves the clients and colleagues who visit the offices with his strange and brooding presence, the lawyer tries to dismiss him. Bartleby, however, "prefers" to stay. When the lawyer then moves to new offices, leaving Bartleby alone in the empty room, the suite's new residents implore the narrator to return to the building to help them get rid of Bartleby, who lurks in the stairwell but refuses the lawyer's offers to help him find a new job or even to reside temporarily in the lawyer's home. To these entreaties, Bartleby only replies, "I would prefer not to." When Bartleby is finally arrested for vagrancy and imprisoned, the lawyer visits him and pays the guards to look after him, but when the narrator returns, he finds Bartleby alone in the grassy prison yard, lying curled up on his side, facing the wall, dead.

As readers may have already surmised, the longer I worked with Mondale, the more I began to see him as my Bartleby. Identifying with the well-meaning attorney, I found myself, like him, intrigued, frustrated, and ultimately befuddled by this person in my charge who rebuffed what I saw as my sincere efforts to help him. I submit to this unflattering parallel to suggest that both stories (Melville's and my own) are instructive to those who aspire to teach for social justice. For although Melville's lawyer is, by his own account, a principled, patient, and ethically attentive man, Melville affords his readers enough interpretive freedom to see the lawyer's individual blind spots and the social complexities that hinder even his most earnest efforts to do the right—the just—thing. The same is true, I think, for my work with Mondale, and in what follows I discuss what he taught me about some of the issues I believe educators will inevitably face as we consider the future of teaching for social justice: the difficulty of defining even our most hallowed principles, the complexities involved in work that requires the participation of those we seek to help, and the potential benefits of alternative models of democracy for supporting social justice teaching. In this way, I enter what sj Miller, in her introduction to this book, calls a "fourthspace" where I was lead (or, perhaps better said, compelled) to "reflect, reconsider, reconceptualize, rejuvenate, and reengage" in my teaching of Mondale and his classmates (p. 7).

Principled Habits

Early in Melville's story, soon after Bartleby first responds, "I would prefer not to," the narrator asks himself a fundamental question that might as easily be asked by those who aspire to teach for social justice: "What had one best do?" (p. 1333). The question may seem clever or even disingenuous, for definitions of "justice" often seem clear enough. It would be hard to argue, for instance, that forcefully segregating schools by race or ethnicity or that denying gay, lesbian, or transgendered students the right to learn in an environment free from harassment or neglect violate "justice" by almost any reasonable standard. But some people do make such arguments, and in day-to-day life related to schools, many other issues arise that make this question of "what had one best do" difficult to answer with any kind of certainty. What is "just"—school admission based on grades and test scores, or on a more holistic consideration of an applicant's life circumstances? Equal funding of schools by enrollment, or the right of individual communities to determine their own levels of funding based on tax rates they themselves determine? Opening Latino Hope to students of all Chicago neighborhoods and races, or preserving it as a place uniquely hospitable to Latino students? Allowing Mondale to sit wherever he wants and do (or not) the schoolwork he chooses, or insisting that he move in from the hallway and comport himself like the other students in English Three? The debate, therefore, is less about whether we teachers should promote social justice than about what social justice really is. This is the inconvenient point made earlier in this volume by David Kirkland and Danielle Filipiak (2007), who astutely note that one of the challenges of teaching for social justice is that it "varies by situation" (p. 61).

In making this point about the difficulty of defining a principle like "social justice" in educational settings, Kirkland and Filipiak write specifically of a conundrum discussed more generally by Stanley Fish (1999), who argues that the "trouble with principle[s]" is that "there are no neutral principles, only so-called principles . . . . And even if you could come up with a principle that was genuinely neutral . . . it would be unhelpful because it would . . . point you in no particular direction, would not tell you where to go or what to do" (p. 4). But Fish also points out that if allegedly neutral principles are unhelpful in directing particular courses of action, such principles are not benign, for they can be invoked to attach a semblance of disinterested moral authority to decidedly partisan and potentially abhorrent agendas. Fish puts it this way: "The problem is that any attempt to define one of these [abstract principles]—to give it content—will always and necessarily proceed from the vantage point of some currently unexamined assumptions about the way life is or should be" (p. 3). Fish traces the inclination to rely on principles and to leave the assumptions they conceal "unexamined" to the legacy of political liberalism and, specifically, to the thought of John Rawls. As Fish explains, Rawls championed general principles because he believed that the vexing complexity of lived life obscures moral clarity and threatens consistency in what people want to be principled judgments. To Rawls, because a modern society is characterized by such a plurality of competing viewpoints and moral doctrines, the only way to cut through all this diversity of opinion is to "abstract from and not be . . . affected by the contingencies of the moral world" (1993 p. 23, in Fish, 1999, p. 10). Rawls argues that in order to bracket these complexities, to clear away the historical and sociocultural clutter that will keep us from recognizing manifestations of principles like justice, people must willfully don a "veil of ignorance"—ignorance of "features relating to social position, native endowment, and historical accident, as well as the contents of persons' determinate conceptions of good" (1993, p. 79, in Fish, 1999, p. 10).

Would that it were true, as Rawls claimed, that one could achieve principled clarity by emptying the world of contingencies. If so, Melville's narrator, in the name of justice, could have dismissed Bartleby without hesitation rather than struggling for weeks to define what best to do with his idle scrivener. Or, in a gesture of compassion, he might have allowed Bartleby to remain in the law offices rather than abandoning him after hearing "uncharitable remarks" that began to circulate among the lawyer's professional acquaintances regarding the "strange creature" he kept at his office (p. 1346). For my part, I might have upheld a clear standard of "fairness" and demanded that Mondale either drop English Three or sit inside the classroom rather than worrying what his losing an English credit would to do his chances of earning his high school diploma. Unfortunately for the lawyer and me, there was no way to set aside the histories, needs, abilities, and other particularities of Bartleby and Mondale and appeal merely to principles that are untroubled by reality.

The futility of abstracting the principle of social justice from the lives of teachers and students is clear to Danielle Filipiak, who describes her struggles to define "justice" during her semesters as a preservice teacher in this way:

> I just wish they would have provided more support for teachers who wanted to teach for justice in urban areas. Quite frankly, most of us didn't know what the hell justice meant. I wished that my teacher education would have prepared me to define justice so that I didn't have to tuck my education so neatly into a "white" box. (p. 55)

In my view, the essential insight of Filipiak's words is that she asks not that her education professors provide her with a categorical definition of "justice," but that they prepare her to define "justice" on her own terms. Indeed, Filipiak recognizes that "justice" cannot be explained unconditionally in an education manual or a methods course. Rather, she knows, as she and Kirkland write, that "social justice is meaningless unless we make it mean," that such meanings "are located in history," and that they emanate "from specific locales of stories— both ours and others" (p. 61). In looking to the particularities of lived life for clues as to how principles like "social justice" can be transformed into commitments that can be identified and acted upon, Kirkland and Filipiak reflect the thinking of Oliver Wendell Holmes, who, as a Supreme Court justice, asserted that judicial decisions, though they have to be publicly explained in terms of the abstract principles adduced to support them, are in fact arrived at based not on legal logic but on experience. As Louis Menand (2001) explains, by "experience" Holmes meant "everything that arises out of the interaction of humans with their environment: beliefs, sentiments, customs, values, policies, and prejudices—what [Holmes] called 'the felt necessities of the time'" (Menand, 2001, p. 342). Similarly, Fish argues that what we call "principles" are actually preferences based on experience. These preferences are not of a capricious or casual kind, but those that amount to what Fish calls "substantive commitments," which he describes as "strong moral intuitions as to how the world should go combined with the resolve to be faithful to them" (p. 9).

But if we abandon the notion that abstract principles can be defined in any consequential way, and if we accept instead that our "substantive commitments" arise from "the felt necessities of the time," the issue remains as to how teacher educators might best attend to Filipiak's admonition to prepare our students to define and effect social justice. This question goes beyond whether or not the preferences we have in a given situation are the right ones, for to help preservice teachers define "social justice" is not really a matter of definition at all. Rather, it is a question of method: How might we provide opportunities for preservice teachers to encounter and struggle with the very contingencies that "justice" as an abstract principle tends to obscure? I believe that the best answer to that question is to say, first, that teacher educators must make clear to their students that social justice should be at the center of their conceptual framework of what it means to be a good teacher, and second, that preservice teachers should, as often as possible, be placed in situations where they have the chance to develop what I'll call "principled habits" of defining justice for themselves in a variety of contexts. In speaking of principled habits, I follow Dewey's conception of habits as people's "inclinations" to keep learning and growing in a way that affords them the opportunity to productively engage in a changing world (1916/1985, p. 53). Indeed, Dewey (1927/1988) explains that his notion of a "habit" "goes deeper than the ordinary conception of a habit as a more or less fixed way of doing things. It covers the formation of attitudes that are both emotional and intellectual; it includes our basic sensitivities and ways of meeting and responding to all the conditions that we meet in living (p. 35). Thus, the principled habits that are essential to foster in beginning teachers are not those that would lead them to refer resolutely and immovably to a principle, but a way of thinking and acting that leads them to explore what a principle like "justice" or any other might mean amid all the variables of a given context.

In addition to Kirkland and Filipiak, other contributors to this book demonstrate the importance and possibility of providing opportunities for beginning teachers to explore the meaning of social justice pedagogy based on their particular teaching circumstances. Peggy Rice, for instance, writes that she asks her students "to articulate their vision of the future and what they plan to do as a teacher to promote that vision," and that these discussions consist of "critical reflections of our experiences" (p. 70). Similarly, sj Miller writes that "a goal I have in working with preservice teachers is to mentor them through a process of coming to terms with how they activate a pedagogy that not only works for them but also for their students" (p. 97). Miller's student Channell Wilson-Segura affirms the necessity of this process, noting that "social justice is not something that is taught" but that emerges as individuals choose to be morally "embedded" within the "many layers that surround this complex form of activism" (p. 117).

In making a case for principled habits rather than principles, I don't mean to imply that a principle like "social justice" is necessarily useless, for I think invoking it is an essential way to extend and enrich conversations about which priorities should be included in the work of teachers. Neither do I wish to suggest that people are incapable of making substantive and thoughtful decisions, for we make such decisions all the time. Rather, I posit principled habits as a potentially useful concept in discussions about teaching for social justice because there are times when teacher educators can't tell their students what "justice" is any more than I could tell Nancy exactly what she should do (and why) when it was her turn to teach and Mondale dragged his chair into the hallway. What I could and did do, however, was include her in the process of trying figure out what would serve the long-term interests of Mondale and our other students in English Three. This is, to be sure, an uncertain process, one that Fish tells us induces a "moral anxiety" (p. 6), and it leads to no timeless and inviolable right answer. Still, for Nancy and me, it was a process that at once drew upon and developed our principled habits as we engaged in the hard and perpetual work of thoughtfully rummaging through our experience for clues as to what—at that time and in that place—was the "right" or "just" thing to do.

Subjected to Empowerment

By October, Nancy and I continued to be fairly happy with the way things were going in English Three. Although Nancy had to reduce her time at Latino Hope to one day a week due to the demands of her graduate coursework, she remained active in planning for the class, and, on those days when she could be there, she consistently demonstrated her skills as an insightful leader of class discussions. The students were especially engaged in our in-class reading of *Monster*, by Walter Dean Meyers (2000), a story written in the form of a screen play of a boy on trial for his role in a convenience store robbery and murder. As Nancy and I soon learned, the English Three students knew a great deal about the criminal justice system, and they had plenty to say about zealous prosecutors and over-worked public defenders, about prison conditions and the biases built into a system that works against people who are poor or Latino or African American. Erick, for instance, told of how the Chicago Police would pull him and his friends over "for no reason except that we're Mexican" and search their pockets and vehicle. "How can they just do that?" I asked. "Don't they need probable cause?" Erick shook his head, like he was pained by my naiveté. "Todd," he said, "you ain't ever had your ass beat by Five-0 [the police, an allusion to the television series *Hawaii Five-0*], have you?" When I admitted I hadn't, Erik continued. "Well, I have, and so have other people in here. Five-0 does whatever they want." Following Erik, several other students added their own stories of how they or a family member had been victimized by police.

It was after this class that Nancy suggested that she and I bring in news stories of what at the time was an extensive inquiry by local media into the failure of the Chicago Police Department's Office of Professional Standards to thoroughly investigate allegations of systematic misconduct on the part of its officers. After reading and discussing these articles, a student named Patricia came up with the idea of creating a presentation that included a description of citizens' rights and a skit providing instruction on what to do (or not) during encounters with police. Several of the students liked Patricia's idea, and a few weeks later five of them presented the skit to a class of students at a middle school down the street.

The students also told stories refuting the stereotypes implicit in Meyer's title, *Monster,* which is the epithet that the prosecutor in the book levels at the suspect-protagonist during the trial's opening arguments. It is also a name, the students agreed, that often describes the public's perception of urban youth. One morning, for instance, James challenged this stereotype by emphasizing the strong bonds of obligation he had with his friends. Clearly exhausted, James explained that he had been awoken late the night before by a phone call informing him that one of his "boys" had been picked up by the police and needed to be bailed out of jail. James had spent the rest of the night calling and driving around to the homes of about a dozen friends, collecting over a thousand dollars in cash, which he used to bail out his friend at about seven o'clock that morning. He had come straight to school from the Cook County Jail, with a brief stop at Dunkin' Donuts to get a large coffee. James ended his story by rubbing his eyes and saying, "Thug life, it's too much responsibility."

Nancy and I were encouraged by conversations like these, for we saw them as evidence that our students not just learning about things like plot, characterization, and reading strategies, but that they were also critiquing and re-writing denigrating depictions of urban youth, teaching Nancy and me about the realities of a criminal justice system that she and I knew only from TV courtroom dramas or the safety of a jury box, and asserting their voices in ways that approximate the dialogue that Freire writes of in which "the teacher is no longer merely the one-who-teaches, but one who is himself taught in dialogue with students" (p. 80). Thus, in our more optimistic moments, Nancy and I hoped English Three was in some modest ways contributing to the students' growing sense of being active subjects in their own lives, a trend that we viewed as supportive of our broader commitment to promoting social justice.

Meanwhile, Mondale remained in his seat out in the hallway. It's not that he was completely disengaged from the class. When we read sections of *Monster* aloud, for instance, Mondale volunteered to take the part of the trial judge, his words drifting into the room like a voice over. Also, when, during a subsequent unit just before Halloween, we watched the horror movie, *The Ring*, Mondale insisted that I angle the VCR screen toward him enough so that he could see it from his vantage point in the hallway. He then wrote a review of the movie in which he focused on the relationship between the principal character and her boyfriend. Though he refused to read "The Tell Tale Heart," when we as a class talked about paranormal experiences in preparation for writing our own ghost stories, Mondale was fascinated by his Latino classmates' personal and family tales of "brujería," or witchcraft. The next day during writing workshop, Mondale sat in the hallway and composed this narrative of an experience in his basement bedroom, a story he swore is true. I present it here without editing:

> My story is about the things I see that happen that shouldnt because its weird to see images of body and hear them talking and touching on me. At first I thought I was dreaming but I wasnt its real. Things come up to me while Im laying down and they call my name or they touch me. But yesterday while talking about it in school my classmate Marta says it the witch riding my back but I dont understand it. Theres a picture of my Great Grandmother every time I look up at the picture here eyes move the way I move. So I turn it around when I went to sleep the next morning it was face back toward me.

Despite the missing apostrophes, this story is among the examples of Mondale's work that convinced me that he was a smart kid and a capable writer. He also proved to be an enthusiastic reader, as every day he continued to bring with him a copy of the *Sun-Times* to read if what was going on in English Three didn't interest him. Convinced of his potential as a student, one day after class, I asked Mondale to stay behind for a moment to talk. Though I didn't have my tape recorder running, I remember pretty clearly and can reconstruct from notes what I said. It was something like this: "Mondale, you've showed again and again in this class that you're a really good reader and that you have a lot of potential as a writer. You could go to college if you want to, and I can help you do that. I work at the university nearby. I can help you prepare for the ACT and fill out your application. I know people in the financial aid office and can talk to them about arranging for whatever reduction in tuition and fees that you might be eligible for. I can talk to my friends who run the Summer Bridge Program, where you can take classes that get you ready for your first year. I can even work with the Director of the Composition Program to get you into first-year writing classes with instructors who will give you whatever help you need. You can do this, and I can help. Will you let me help you?"

When I finally stopped talking, overtones of urgent sincerity echoed through the room. But Mondale just shrugged and said, "Aw, hell no, Todd." At the time, because my hair is too short to pull, I just said, "Alright, well, if you change your mind, let me know." Later, though, pondering Mondale's refusal to accept help from me that was, in my estimation, so clearly in his interest, I recalled these words from Melville's lawyer regarding Bartleby: "His perverseness seemed ungrateful, considering the undeniable good usage and indulgence he had received from me" (p. 1340).

Part of my frustration arose from the fact that this situation with Mondale wasn't working out according to what I saw as the "grand narrative" of social justice teaching. According to this narrative, teaching for social justice is a struggle of good versus an evil that is manifest in many forms but that is, for the most part, easily recognizable to people of clear mind and conscience. On the side of good are educators who seek to develop their students' potentials as literate persons, who do all they can to foster in young people a democratizing agency that will extend beyond their classrooms to (re)create a more humane and just world. On the side of evil are those who advocate racist, homophobic, and classist forms of injustice that are perpetuated by school policies like tracking, inequitable funding, and *No Child Left Behind* (to name just a few)—all of which emerge from and are reinforced by more broadly oppressive social, political, and economic structures. In order for Mondale's and my narrative to parallel this one, he and I should have been comrades on the side of good. That is, we should have been collaborating to improve his literacy skills so that he could, first, develop a critical awareness of the ways in which the deck of life had been stacked against him; second, imagine alternatives to the struggles he had encountered thus far; and finally, plan and pursue a future he desired for himself. The problem, though, and the early point at which our story went awry, was that Mondale had little interest in enlisting my help to improve his reading ands writing skills or to apply to college. Again, it wasn't that Mondale was sabotaging English Three by, say, snatching pencils from other students' hands or interrupting people when they were trying to make a point. Rather, he just wasn't doing things that he preferred not to do, like sit inside the classroom or complete most of his schoolwork. Given Mondale's ongoing behavior, I was sure that Melville's lawyer would have understood my plight, having said as he did in reference to Bartleby, "Nothing so aggravates an earnest person as a passive resistance" (p. 1335).

According to Barbara Cruikshank (1999), such passivity presents a special problem for those driven by a "will to empower" people like Mondale (or Bartleby) with the agency of democratic citizenship. Cruikshank argues that "democratic citizens are not born," but are produced by means of what she calls "technologies of citizenship," which she defines as "discourses, programs, and other tactics aimed at making individuals politically active and capable of self-government" (p. 1). Examples of these technologies include a neighborhood organizing campaign, a substance abuse program, and other initiatives promoting self-sufficiency or self-esteem. Central to Cruikshank's argument is that technologies of citizenship are usually not set forth or mandated by the state. Rather, they are present throughout a society as specific strategies of what she calls "governance"—those "forms of action and relations of power that aim to guide and shape (rather than force, control or dominate) the actions of others," including the ways that people act upon themselves (p. 4). Though technologies of citizenship are designed and implemented in a spirit of good will, and though they often do improve the circumstances of those whom they are intended to help, they work only if the voluntary compliance of the "disempowered" can be secured. Thus, in Cruikshank's analysis, passivity is a problem because people's acquiring agency or empowerment requires their cooperation by assenting to the requirements of citizenship.

Cruikshank thus sees citizenship less as a solution to political problems than as a necessary strategy of government in modern, liberal democracies. Absent tyranny, her reasoning goes, people need to think and act for themselves, and technologies of citizenship make it possible for people to promote their own and the general welfare within a given sociopolitical context. However, Cruikshank also contends that when people voluntarily adhere to a technology of citizenship, they are at once empowering themselves and submitting to a means of correcting their alleged deficiencies as citizens. Cruikshank puts it this way: "I see technologies of citizenship, however well intentioned, as modes of constituting and regulating citizens: that is, [as] strategies for governing the very subjects whose problems they seek to redress—the powerless, the apathetic, or those at risk" (p. 2). By positing technologies of citizenship as simultaneously empowering and constraining, as "voluntary and coercive at the same time" (p. 4), Cruikshank follows Foucault (1983) in using the word "subject" in a double sense. On one hand, a "subject" is someone who has the ability and opportunity to do things—to exercise agency over her own or another's life. On the other, a "subject" is one who is subjected to the authority of others. Or, as Cruikshank puts it, by refusing to separate these two necessary aspects of the subject, Foucault uncovers "how modern forms of power tie the subjectivity (conscience, identity, self-knowledge) of the individual to that individual's subjection (control by another)" (p. 212, in Cruikshank, 1999, p. 21).

Though Cruiksank doesn't say so directly, her examples of technologies of citizenship could very well include schools, for they require the cooperation of individuals whom they are designed to empower and thereby position students as "subjects" in both senses of the word. Indeed, among my aims in English Three was to help Mondale acquire the literacy skills that I was convinced he needed to be the author (the subject) of his own life story. I wanted him to have options; I wanted him to be able to decide whether or not to attend college or to choose a job that he liked and was good at without being limited by his abilities to read and write. But I also wanted him to bring his desk in from the hallway and do his schoolwork. Thus, what was less clear to me at the time but has become more apparent since then is that the cost of the agency that I wished for Mondale would, for that semester anyway, have included his subjecting himself to whatever institutional authority I embodied as his teacher. That was a price that Mondale, for his own reasons, preferred not to pay. While I still think that Mondale would probably have been better off in the long run if he had done what I told him to do, and while I believe that his successes as a student and citizen would have served the interests of social justice, I suspect that one of the reasons Mondale wasn't interested in my plans for him was that he recognized better than I did that the "technologies of citizenship" I was proposing he assent to would eliminate other choices he had about what he wanted to do and who he wished to be—choices that, in retrospect, it might have been "just" for me to honor more than I did at the time.

Beyond providing a way to consider Mondale's refusal to assent to things he preferred not to do, Cruikshank's discussion of technologies of citizenship also offers a broader way for educators to think about their work in that her insights complicate what I earlier called the "grand narrative" of social justice teaching. As Laura Bolf Beliveau, Kristen Holzer, and Stephanie Schmidt, have noted earlier in this book, such narratives "can both harm and heal and can thwart or sustain an agenda of social justice" (p. 25). Cruikshank's revision of this overarching story comes from her astute Foucauldan analyses, which in my view are more grounded and nuanced than the traditional account of a "good vs. evil" power struggle between those who have it and those who don't, a dichotomy that has existed at least since Freire distinguished between the "oppressor" and the "oppressed" and that lives on in discourses of social justice that posit liberation as the aspiration of individual or group agents in a struggle with dominant and dominating sociopolitical structures. To be sure, one need not look far to find clear examples of oppression. Nonetheless, by showing that any adoption or exercise of authority is possible only by those who subject themselves to certain kinds of power relations, Cruikshank reconstructs this familiar framework. She blurs the lines of the struggle for agency by conceptualizing power as more than a problem to be solved or the antithesis of freedom (p. 21). Rather, to Cruikshank, power simply "is" in the sense that it is present within the contours of the mundane and in all strata of a society, operating, for better or worse, in ways that cannot always be rationally used or intentionally directed. This does not mean that people should respond to misuses of power with indifference. Nor does it mean that we should abandon our principled habits and shrink from a struggle to rectify both flagrant injustices and those that we thoughtfully uncover. But it does mean, I think, that as the matrices of power multiply and the networks through which it is exercised become ever more diverse, teachers for social justice must consider these complexities and seek to understand the ways in which they serve as either a help or a hindrance as we act on our will to empower.

Democratic Alternatives

Among the leitmotifs of "Bartleby the Scrivener" is that Melville's narrator continually hopes, against accumulating experience, that Bartleby will eventually be reasonable. When Bartleby first announces that he would prefer not to proofread some documents, the lawyer says, "I began to reason with him," asserting that this was a request "made of common usage and according to common sense" (p. 1334). After Bartleby refuses to review yet another set of papers, the narrator wonders, "What added thing is there, perfectly reasonable, that he will be sure to refuse to do?" and he also ponders how anyone, faced with Bartleby's indifference, could "refrain from bitterly exclaiming upon such perverseness—such unreasonableness?" (p. 1337). Finally, in a last appeal before attempting to dismiss Bartleby, the lawyer gently pleads, "Say now, that in a day or two you will begin to be a little reasonable—say so, Bartleby." The scrivener's reply is by now predictable: "At present I would prefer not to be a little reasonable" (p. 1341).

Such appeals to reason are, in effect, appeals to specific ways of thinking and problem solving that characterize the deliberative form of democracy that has been the primary model for efforts to teach for social justice. When Melville's lawyer appeals to Bartleby's reason, he is proposing an informed conversation similar to that which Dewey contends will result in people's discovering and then collectively pursuing what they will likely find to be their common interests. Indeed, deliberative democracy is based on the notion that people talking reasonably to each other can identify and overcome obstacles and injustices, with individuals developing and employing their unique potentials in connection with others toward the benefit of society at large. This rational and informed model is what Dewey (1927/1988) was talking about when he argued that restoring America as a "great community" will require "free social inquiry . . . wedded to the art of full and moving communication" (p. 350). However, deliberative democracy, which, again, has been the dominant model in academic settings for effecting social justice, is subject to critiques that reveal its limitations, and in thinking about the future of social justice teaching, educators need to consider the viability of the deliberative model and explore alternatives to it.

One such critique is that the requirements of deliberative democracy, though appealing in theory, are evasive in practice. As Diana Mutz (2006) has noted, the conditions for realizing a truly deliberative context are similar to those of Habermas's "ideal speech situation" (1989), and they include the equal status of the interlocutors, arguments being carefully constructed and justified in a context of mutual respect, and an eventual consensus. The problem, Mutz argues, is that these conditions are unlikely to occur in real contexts (p. 4). If Mutz is right, then the quintessentially deliberative scenario of people sharing ideas in conversation, behaving well, and adhering to the rules of discussion until a reasonable consensus is reached, is essentially a myth.

Moreover, in addition to casting doubt on the likelihood of circumstances adequate to deliberation as it has been theorized, Mutz challenges the common assumption that deliberative and participatory democracy are mutually supportive. Drawing on recent data that surprised her and many other political scientists, Mutz provides strong evidence that, contrary to intuition, Americans who are most often exposed to ideas that differ from their own—a hallmark of deliberation—are the least likely to be politically active (pp. 32-33). This political inertia, Mutz further shows, is the result either of people's ambivalence regarding controversial issues or of their reluctance to get into arguments with friends and acquaintances (p. 121). Mutz's unsettling findings merit the attention of teachers concerned with social justice, for they disturb not only Dewey's idea of "democracy through conversation" but also Freire's assertion that positive social change can be achieved through a *praxis* arising from dialogue (p. 79)—two notions that have long been prominent in the thought of social justice educators.

Yet another critique of deliberative democracy is articulated by Aaron Schutz, who, in an important and provocative series of essays exploring the question of whether schools can "empower" students and promote democracy (2001a, 2001b, in press), suggests that the allegedly neutral and reasonable nature of deliberative democracy in fact conceals a middle-class bias. Schutz (in press) contends that deliberative democracy emerges from what he calls "discursive collaboration," a conceptual and communicative framework that relies on and privileges self-monitoring, individuality, abstract reasoning, high mobility, and relatively weak social ties that can be dissolved and recreated as the circumstances for deliberation demand. Because these cultural patterns are most common among middle- and upper-middle-class managers, analysts, and educators, Schutz argues that in the early twentieth century, it was this discursive model that became ascendant in colleges of education, where it eclipsed educational ideals and priorities that might otherwise have emerged from the working class. The legacy of this development, Schutz writes, continues today, leading him to observe that "it is not an exaggeration to say that schools are one of the most unlikely places in our society for members of the middle and working classes to meet on equal terms" (in press).

But if the discursive cultural pattern of schools silences students from working class cultures, if it ignores what these students know and excludes them from discussions of how best to discover and promote ways of teaching that foster social justice, the resultant, contrived consensus should come as no surprise. For as Chantal Mouffe (2000) asserts in a critique of deliberative democracy, "consensus in a liberal-democratic society is—and always will be—the expression of a hegemony and the crystallization of power relations" (p. 49). Carrying the weight of hegemonic power concealed in the unremarkable and innocently reasonable form of deliberative democracy, schools may thus be said often to pursue education not as means of promoting social justice, but as a way of changing people to think like middle-class individuals do. And if anyone resists, even passively, preferring not to assimilate, his only option is self-banishment from the "great community" that Dewey describes. Bartleby ends up alone in a prison yard; Mondale, in the hallway; Damon, in a refrigerator box.

Wary of the homogenizing and alienating tendencies of deliberative democracy, Schutz argues that modes of social interaction holding greater potential for effecting justice can be found in the traditions of the working class. In contrast to the middle class orientation of "discursive collaboration," Schutz writes that working class people tend to demonstrate a mode of social interaction that he calls "organic solidarity," which responds to the cultural practices and limited monetary resources specific to working-class life, and which emphasizes the importance of interpersonal relationships, "straight talk," and "solving problems head on as opposed to placating and long discussions" (in press). Schutz calls the strategy of activism that emerges from this orientation "democratic solidarity," and he traces its methods, which involve seeking out native leaders who meet with groups of people and then gather to formulate strategies for collective action, back to the labor and community organizing tactics pioneered by Saul Alinski. Schutz argues that this organic form of action is, in reality, far more democratic than the deliberative one because the working-class model forces changes that have direct material benefit to people who are poor or otherwise oppressed. In looking beyond schools and their attendant frameworks of deliberative democracy for resources in the pursuit of justice, Schutz joins Jean Anyon (2006), who urges educational researchers to pay special attention to "opportunity structures and policies existing outside of schools" and to "successful methods of organizing and building power within communities" (pp. 21 & 23). Thus, to both Schutz and Anyon, the time has come to forgo ineffective strategies of action that rely primarily on talking and to get busy, as Schutz puts it, "wrestling power from others who will generally not give it up without a fight" (in press).

The organic, community-based model of democracy endorsed by both Schutz and Anyon increases the range of options for teachers who have made social justice their priority. First, by emphasizing inclusive human relationships rather than narrow standards of "reasonableness," this model puts forward a way to include in democratizing action people (like Bartleby or Mondale) whom we might otherwise ignore because they prefer not to think and act like us; and second, it justifies a vigorous, perhaps even unyielding stance toward people with whom we disagree. I'm thinking, now, of a few people in particular: a teacher I know who resents the presence of English language learners in his classroom and denies his responsibility to educate them; the state legislator I met who opposes tax reforms that would ameliorate the "savage inequalities" in school funding; the guy who lives down the block, who, at a recent neighborhood association meeting, argued strenuously against a proposal for mixed-income housing in our ward. Though deliberating with these people increased my understanding of the rationales for the views they hold, the longer I talked to them, the more I was convinced that they were wrong.

With Schutz and Anyon, Fish responds to such situations by advocating a more contentious means of effecting change than can be derived from a deliberative model. After solemnly raising Rawls's question of whether, "given the deep oppositions that have always divided [people] along religious, philosophical, and moral lines, just cooperation among free and equal citizens is possible'" (p. 4, in Fish, 1999, p. 12), Fish replies in a way that for him is characteristically blunt: "It isn't." What is possible, Fish contends, is "cooperation achieved through the give and take of substantive agendas as they via for the right to be supreme over this or that part of the political landscape" (p. 12). Mouffe (1993), though she shares Fish's general sentiments, articulates them more forcefully than he does by advocating a model of radical democracy characterized chiefly by what she calls "agonistic pluralism," which requires "a vibrant clash of political positions and an open conflict of interests" (p. 6). In accepting this non-deliberative model, then, a teacher who presumes to make social justice among her personal and professional priorities must embrace and tolerate a paradox of values. One the one hand, she must be driven by a communitarian desire to discover and effect strategies that bring people together, and she must seek to establish critically empathic relationships that inform and motivate efforts directed toward ends that all parties agree are humane and just. On the other hand, she must be wary of consensus, guard against its potential to eradicate diverse views and perpetuate injustice, and, in the end, be prepared to organize, dig in, and not budge until she gets her way.

My point in describing these critiques of deliberative democracy is not to suggest that it be jettisoned as a way to strive for justice. For years, I myself have used a deliberative (specifically, Deweyan) framework to think and talk about schools, and I still believe it provides a useful way to describe both the means and ends of democratic education. Moreover, I think that some of the aspects of the organic or agonistic alternatives I've mentioned here include significant aspects of deliberation, even if these are downplayed or given another name. Still, although the deliberative model has served us well, and though it has not yet outlived its usefulness, as Ruth Vinz has noted in her preface to this volume, often, "when the actual school day begins, the pressures may overwhelm our best intentions and blur the theoretical lenses through which we engage with social justice, civic rights, difference, and equality" (p. xxii). Insofar as the "theoretical lense" of deliberative democracy grows increasingly "blurred," it is important to search for alternative models of democracy that will help us articulate and maintain our present and future commitments to teaching for social justice. Mouffe encourages us to just that, noting that in a changing world, traditional forms of democracy may be inadequate, and that we are therefore charged with imagining and creating new forms of democracy, forms that "should be plural and adapted to the type of social relations where democratic principles of liberty and equality are implemented" (p. 104). Similarly, Michael Hardt and Antonio Negri (2004) write optimistically of an emerging global "multitude" that, "composed of innumerable internal differences. . . disperses trends to unitary sovereignty," and that, in its potential for constant reorganization, makes new forms of democracy and its attendant forms of justice possible (pp. xiv & 340). As these writers help us see, democracy is always in flux, and amid those changes lies the possibility of discovering new and perhaps better ways to describe and work effectively toward those things we care so deeply about.

Not Quitting

In the introduction to a recent collection of essays about educational research in the interests of social justice (Ladson-Billings and Tate, 2006), Gloria Ladson-Billings writes with eloquent frustration of the spectacle of injustice that was the aftermath of Hurricane Katrina. Ladson-Billings—an icon of social justice education, a scholar who has devoted her career to struggling against the kinds of willful ignorance and inertia that would create conditions wherein people would be left drowning, homeless, or sweltering in a fetid sports arena—writes this to educators who, with her, witnessed what happened in New Orleans when the winds blew, the levees broke, and the water swept away whatever veneer of justice lay over the city:

> Hurricane Katrina brings shame upon us all. We have no excuse for our ignorance about poverty. We cannot keep writing about schools as some idyllic, romantic places where a few students are failing. The work we have to do must be done in the public interest. We cannot hide behind notions of neutrality or objectivity when people are suffering so desperately. The questions we pursue, the projects we choose, the agenda

we champion have to . . . matter in the lives of real people . . . . It is just too bad that
we have had to have a disaster to make this clear to us. (p. 10)

As I did, readers might imagine Ladson-Billings as she writes these words,
removing her hands from the keyboard and gripping the edges of her desk as
she blinks from her eyes tears of rage and grief. Those of us who care about
educating for social justice—and about sharing that priority with future
generations of teachers—might also join Ladson-Billings in her response of
anger and exasperation to ongoing evidence of injustice that seems hopelessly
entrenched. Further, we might grow discouraged by our own limitations in
pursuing social justice in our work. That is, we might recognize in ourselves a
bit of Melville's narrator—his feelings of puzzlement and pity, his inability to
emerge from his established and insufficient ways of thinking, his futile
protestations of good intentions, his stubborn unwillingness to do anything that
would imperil his desire to remain an "eminently *safe* man" (p. 1328, original
italics).

But whatever anxieties emerge from our imperfect efforts to teach for
social justice, these feelings arise not only from our own, personal limitations.
It is no accident that Melville gives to his tale the subtitle, "A Story of Wall
Street," for in these words is the recognition that the lawyer is but one
individual whose imagination and actions are constrained by the economic and
social structures that surround him. His failure, in other words, is emblematic of
the difficulty of individual efforts toward justice in the absence of broader
change. Moreover, in addition to the institutional vastness of injustice,
individual teachers might also become weary upon realizing that teaching for
justice is an undertaking that never ends. As Melville's lawyer says of Bartleby:
"*he was always there*—first in the morning, continually through the day, and the
last at night" (p. 1337, original italics). Likewise, for me, Mondale was always
there, every day in English Three, squeezing past me in the hallway between
classes. Even when the term ended and Mondale moved on to take classes to
prepare for his GED test, other students who at once illustrated the need for
social justice teaching and the challenges that arise from it continued to show
up in my classroom. And they always will. Melville's lawyer tired of it all, finally
asking Bartleby, "Will you, or will you not, quit me?" Bartleby's response,
echoing in countless voices, is this: "I would prefer *not* to quit you" (p. 1344,
original italics).

Indeed, those who suffer from injustice—and that includes us all, whether
we realize it or not—will never quit us. I confess that in this concluding
chapter, I haven't offered clear instructions as to exactly how to meet that
perpetual responsibility, or to enjoy the opportunity to try. I do this not to be
coy, but to invite readers to discover their own answers in the stories collected

in this book. For as Clifford Geertz (1973) explains concerning all interpretive writing, its aim "is not to answer our deepest questions, but to make available to others answers that others . . . have given, and thus include them in the consultable record of what [has been] said" (p. 30). I'll presume for a moment to speak for all the contributors to this book and say that our hope is that readers will reflect on our stories to inspire and inform their own accounts that can be added to the "consultable record of what has been said" about teaching for social justice. As we tell and hear these stories, as we use them to help ourselves lift the veil of ignorance and see as best we can the world in all its fluid complexity and detail, we will, I suspect, affirm that *whatever* solutions with which we respond to injustice must be of our own making. Such responses will be contextualized, provisional, agile, even as our commitment to justice does not waiver.

References

Anyon, J. (2006). What should count as educational research: Toward a new paradigm. In Ladson-Billings, G. & Tate, W. (Eds.), *Education research in the public interest: Social justice, action, and policy* (pp. 17-26). New York: Teachers College Press.

Cruikshank, B. (1999). *The will to empower: Democratic citizens and other subjects.* Ithaca: Cornell University Press.

Dewey, J. (1916/1985). *Democracy and education.* Boydston, J. (Ed.), *John Dewey, the middle works works: 1899-1924, vol. 9* (pp. 4-370). Carbondale and Edwardsville: Southern Illinois University Press.

Dewey, J. (1927/1988). *The public and its problems.* Boydston, J. (Ed.), In *John Dewey, the later works: 1925-1953, vol. 2* (pp. 235-372). Carbondale and Edwardsville: Southern Illinois University Press.

Fecho, B. (2004). *Is this English? Race, language, and culture in the classroom.* New York: Teachers College Press.

Fish, S. (1999). *The trouble with principle.* Cambridge: Harvard University Press.

Foucault, M. (1983). The subject and power. In Dreyfus, H. & Rabinow, P. (Eds.), *Michel Foucault: Beyond structuralism and hermeneutics,* (2nd ed., pp. 208-228). Chicago: University of Chicago Press.

Freire, P. (1970/2002). *Pedagogy of the oppressed.* New York: Continuum

Geertz, C. (1973). *The interpretation of cultures.* New York: Basic Books.

Greene, M. (1988). *The dialectic of freedom.* New York: Teachers College Press.

Habermas, J. (1989). *The structural transformation of the public sphere.* Cambridge: MIT Press.

Hardt, M. & Negri, A. (2004). *Multitude: War and democracy in the age of empire.* New York: Penguin.

Hawaii Five-0 Homepage. (2007). URL: http://www.mjq.net/fiveo/

Ladson-Billings, G. & Tate, W. (Eds.) (2006). *Education research in the public interest: Social justice, action, and policy.* New York: Teachers College Press.

Melville, H. (1856/1980). Bartleby the scivener. In McMichael. G. (Ed.), *Anthology of American literature, Vol. 1: Colonial through Romantic* (2nd ed., pp. 1328-1352). New York: Macmillan.

Menand, L. (2001). *The metaphysical club.* New York: Farrar, Straus, and Giroux.

Meyers, W. (2000). *Monster.* New York: Scholastic Books.

Mouffe, C. (1993). *The return of the political.* London & New York: Verso.

Mouffe, C. (2000). *The democratic paradox.* London & New York: Verso.

Mutz, D. (2006). *Hearing the other side: Deliberative versus participatory democracy.* Cambridge: Cambridge University Press.

Rawls, J. (1993). *Political liberalism.* New York: Columbia University Press.

Schutz, A. (2001a). John Dewey's conundrum: Can democratic schools empower? *Teachers College Record, 103* (2), 267-302.

Schutz, A. (2001b). John Dewey and a 'paradox of size': Democratic faith at the limits of experience. *American Journal of Education, 109* (May), 287-319.

Schutz, A. (in press). Social class and social action: The middle class bias of democratic theory in education. *Teachers College Record.* 110 (2).

Contributors

Alena Bogucki earned a BS in Secondary Education at Ball State University in May 2006 and began graduate studies during the summer 2007. She currently enjoys facilitating a vibrant learning environment for her ninth and tenth grade Language Arts students and informing her methodology via participation in the National Council for the Teachers of English (NCTE) and Women in Literacy and Life Assembly (WILLA); she is also the Ball State Teachers College Alumni Association Secretary and a Teacher-Consultant for the Indiana Writing Project.

Laura Bolf Beliveau is Assistant Professor and English Education Program Coordinator at the University of Central Oklahoma. She taught high school English in urban, rural, and suburban districts in Illinois, Iowa, and Wisconsin. Laura's research interests include emotional responses to teaching and the development of teacher identities, especially as they intersect with issues of diversity and social justice.

Todd DeStigter is a former high school teacher who is now an English educator at the University of Illinois at Chicago. His principal scholarly interests are secondary English teacher education, urban literacies, the ways in which teaching and learning can promote democratic thought and action, and the social and political philosophy of John Dewey. Recently, Todd has taught courses in the methods of teaching English, the uses of literacy in a multicultural democracy, and the contributions of American pragmatism to progressive education. Most of his recent publications are based on the ethnographic research he conducts at a Chicago alternative high school for "at risk" students.

Danielle Filipiak is a seventh grade English teacher at University Preparatory Academy in Detroit, MI. She holds an MA in Curriculum and Teaching from Michigan State University and has presented innovative teaching techniques and projects that put students' voices and experiences at the center of the classroom. She serves as an active member of the Michigan Council for the Teachers of English and Allied Media Conference. Her work with students strives to develop a political and social consciousness through critical dialogue, community interaction, and diverse experiences.

Jamey Katen is a 2003 graduate of Ball State University and has a degree in Elementary Education with a concentration in Language Arts. She is currently working on her Master of Arts in Education with a Reading Specialty License. She has taught elementary school for four years. Her first two years of teaching, she taught fourth grade in Calumet City, Illinois. For the past two years, she taught second grade at small private school in Columbus, Ohio. She has moved to Raleigh, North Carolina and will begin her fifth year, teaching fourth grade in Durham Public Schools.

Emily Marie Keifer graduated from Ball State University with a degree in Elementary Education in May of 2007. She has accepted a position as the 5th-6th grade reading teacher at a small Midwestern school district and is excitedly preparing for her first year of teaching.

David E. Kirkland is Assistant Professor of English Education at New York University. His research interests focus on youth culture, language and literacy studies, African American studies, and urban teacher education. He taught secondary reading and English language arts for five years in two major Michigan cities. Currently, he is writing two books: *A Search Past Silence: Exploring Literacy in the Life of a Young Black Man* and *The Promise in their Eyes: Using Youth Culture to Teach Secondary English* (with others).

Kristy Lorenzo grew up in Kane, Pennsylvania with her mother and younger brother and lived near to her father and grandparents. She attended Indiana University of Pennsylvania and earned a degree in English Education. She completed student teaching in Indiana Area School District, graduated, and worked as a substitute teacher for several months. She is passionate about teaching English and staying current with new approaches and trends in the field, and is eager to continue her education in the near future. In addition to her interests in teaching English, she enjoys reading, especially mysteries and feminist literature. She also likes to play golf, snowboard, watch movies, and spend time with her family and pets.

Kristen Ogilvie Holzer is a doctoral student in Educational Studies at the University of Oklahoma. Her research interests include narrative theory made manifest through ludic pedagogy against the backdrop of secondary coeducation and the moral implications of aesthetic play.

sj Miller is Assistant Professor of Secondary English Education at Indiana University of Pennsylvania. sj has published widely in journals and, most notably, won the 2005 Article of the Year Award from the *English Journal* for "Shattering Images of Violence in Young Adult Literature: Strategies for the Classroom." Most recently sj published (co-authored with Linda Norris) *Unpacking the Loaded*

Teacher Matrix: Negotiating Space and Time Between University and Secondary English Classrooms which received the Richard A. Meade award from NCTE. Current research interests are in unpacking English teacher identity in spacetime as pre-service teachers experience the larger matrix of the teaching world.

Peggy Rice, an Associate Professor of English Education at Ball State University, is a former elementary school teacher. For the past few years she has taught children's literature and a senior seminar focusing on trends and issues in the teaching of Elementary English Language Arts. Her research focuses on critical literacy with preservice elementary teachers, practicing elementary teachers, and children. She is especially interested in understanding how children's literature written from diverse perspectives can deepen understanding of others in order to dispel stereotypes and move toward a more equitable society.

Stephanie Schmidt graduated with a B.A. in English from Luther College in 2005. She is currently a master's and certification student in English Education at the University of Oklahoma. She plans on student teaching and finishing her thesis in the spring of 2008. Stephanie has a newfound passion for all things involving young adult literature. She looks forward to being able to apply this passion in the classroom.

Channell Wilson-Segura is a native of culturally enriched Santa Fe, New Mexico, and resides with her husband Matthew and their two children, Nevada and Cole. Influenced by her senior English teacher, and a love of literature and the performing arts, Channell pursued her bachelor's degree in English and dance at the University of New Mexico. Realizing an intrinsic drive to teach and be a positive influence on the youth of her community, Channell began her graduate studies in secondary education. Upon graduation, she accepted a job from her alma mater, Capital High School. By observing the lack in academic motivation and the low literacy levels of the students she teaches from year to year, she makes a conscious effort to engage her students by modeling her love of literature and teaches them how to analyze literature beyond the writing on the pages in front of them. More importantly, she focuses on the development of a safe-to-learn environment in her classroom and builds positive, lasting relationships with her students, which in turn makes them productive, engaged students. She hopes to further her studies focusing on influencing positive and progressive systemic change by transitioning into administration later in her career, but feels she is currently needed in the classroom working one-on-one with her students. She believes that there is a spirit in the teenager that is resilient and technical on a level that is challenging and promotes growth in her own being that she has never before been enlightened to.

Ruth Vinz is a Professor in English Education at Teachers College, Columbia University and holds the Enid and Lester Morse Endowed Chair in Teacher Education. She taught high school for twenty-three years before becoming a teacher educator. She is the author of numerous articles and thirteen books on ELA curriculum, assessment, and instruction, including *Composing a Teaching Life* which received one of the CEE Richard Meade awards for outstanding research in English Education. Her scholarship and teaching focus on understanding how, when, or why learning happens and how multiple literacies shape those engagements. She examines what teaching practices and aspects of school culture create responsive pedagogies and how those promote teacher and student learning. The end goal is to understand how we do and might create learning environments that provoke intellectual possibility, the capacity to wonder, to dream, to imagine, to disturb, to question, and to take action in the world.

INDEX

Studies in the Postmodern Theory of Education

General Editors
Joe L. Kincheloe & Shirley R. Steinberg

Counterpoints publishes the most compelling and imaginative books being written in education today. Grounded on the theoretical advances in criticalism, feminism, and postmodernism in the last two decades of the twentieth century, Counterpoints engages the meaning of these innovations in various forms of educational expression. Committed to the proposition that theoretical literature should be accessible to a variety of audiences, the series insists that its authors avoid esoteric and jargonistic languages that transform educational scholarship into an elite discourse for the initiated. Scholarly work matters only to the degree it affects consciousness and practice at multiple sites. Counterpoints' editorial policy is based on these principles and the ability of scholars to break new ground, to open new conversations, to go where educators have never gone before.

For additional information about this series or for the submission of manuscripts, please contact:

Joe L. Kincheloe & Shirley R. Steinberg
c/o Peter Lang Publishing, Inc.
29 Broadway, 18th floor
New York, New York 10006

To order other books in this series, please contact our Customer Service Department:

(800) 770-LANG (within the U.S.)
(212) 647-7706 (outside the U.S.)
(212) 647-7707 FAX

Or browse online by series:
www.peterlang.com